I0408838

EIR (ISSN 0273-6314) *is published weekly
(50 issues), by EIR News Service, Inc.,
P.O. Box 17390, Washington, D.C. 20041-0390.
(703) 297-8434*

European Headquarters: E.I.R. GmbH, Postfach
Bahnstrasse 9a, D-65205, Wiesbaden, Germany
Tel: 49-611-73650
Homepage: http://www.eir.de
e-mail: info@eir.de
Director: Georg Neudecker

Montreal, Canada: 514-461-1557
eir@eircanada.ca

Denmark: EIR - Danmark, Sankt Knuds Vej 11,
basement left, DK-1903 Frederiksberg, Denmark.
Tel.: +45 35 43 60 40, Fax: +45 35 43 87 57. e-mail:
eirdk@hotmail.com.

Mexico City: EIR, Sor Juana Inés de la Cruz 242-2
Col. Agricultura C.P. 11360
Delegación M. Hidalgo, México D.F.
Tel. (5525) 5318-2301
eirmexico@gmail.com

Raising Mankind's Standard: The Eurasian Land-Bridge

EDITORIALS

The New Silk Road Opens A New Perspective for Mankind

by Helga Zepp-LaRouche, chairwoman of the German political party
Civil Rights Movement Solidarity (*BüSo*)

May 5—It's unfair to the German people: Strategically there is an epochal change for the better underway, yet the citizens of this country find themselves in the valley of the clueless—thanks to a *de facto* news embargo, imposed by the politicians and the media, which prevents the people from realizing the potential it holds for Germany.

Chinese President Xi Jinping's initiative—the New Silk Road, also called the Belt and Road Initiative—has developed an unprecedented dynamic since he proclaimed it a good three and a half years ago. More than a hundred countries and international organizations are now participating in the greatest infrastructure and development program in history, a program that has developed into the true motor of the world economy.

On May 14-15 in Beijing, a major conference, the Belt and Road Forum, will consolidate this project of the century, with the participation of 28 heads of state and government, more than 150 leading figures from international organizations, and 1,200 high-ranking representatives from 110 countries. This conference will make clear to the whole world that a fully new set of values has emerged in the world, in which a higher level of cooperation between nations, for the common interests of mankind, is superseding the geopolitical interests of individual countries or groups of countries.

Meanwhile, China has concluded 130 bilateral and regional transportation agreements, has initiated 356 international routes for passengers and freight, and has opened 4,200 direct flight connections with 43 countries. There are 39 rail routes currently in operation between China and Europe. A freight train leaves Chongqing every day *en route* to Europe. Six major transport and development corridors between Asia and Europe are under construction as well as an entirely new rail network in Eastern and Central Africa. And the maritime Silk Road for the 21st Century is also being built. This is only the beginning of an initiative that is open to the participation of every nation on the planet.

The world community is currently divided in two: One side grasps this idea, and the other is clinging to the old, obsolete ideas of geopolitics. That may be difficult for German citizens to understand, because the politicians and media conceal these crucial developments from them, and instead deliver an indigestible cocktail of fake news, commentary, and irrelevant distractions.

The May 3 address of American Secretary of State Rex Tillerson to the State Department staff has great strategic significance in this connection. He not only affirmed President Trump's election promise that the United States will no longer conduct regime change interventions into other nations to impose its own so-called values, but he also stressed several times that the United States is working with China to define their relationship for the next 50 years, and that this represents an enormous opportunity.

Chinese Ambassador Cui Tiankai invited the United States—in his speech to the International Finance and Infrastructure Cooperation Forum in New York City on April 24—to join in the Silk Road initiative, the Belt and Road, which would open up great potential for American enterprise. Cui expressed his hope that the United States would seize the initiative and participate in the Belt and Road Forum on May 14-15 in Beijing. President Xi Jinping stressed, during his visit to Mar-a-Lago, Florida in early April, that there are thousands of reasons for the Chinese-American relationship to be a success, and not one for it to break down.

China's *Global Times* later made fun of a series of articles in the *New York Times* that totally missed the mark in interpreting the relationship between the U.S. and Chinese heads of state. It noted that in articles with titles such as "Why Trump's Budding Bromance with Xi is Doomed" and "Trump Is a Chinese Agent," the *New York Times* could scarcely conceal its acid sarcasm, but that in the *Global Times'* view it had long since been overtaken by the new era.

In fact, it appears that in the editorial offices of the mainstream media, the dress code does not permit the wearing of concave glasses to correct for myopia.

Embracing the Historic Opportunity

In contrast to similar backward-looking politicians in Germany, Japan has recognized the opportunity inherent in Japan's cooperation with the Silk Road Initiative. Several high-ranking Japanese figures will participate in the May summit, for example, Toshihiro Nikai, the General Secretary of the ruling Liberal Democratic Party (LDP), who is known for his pro-China views and is number two in the party after Prime Minister Shinzo Abe; Trade Minister Hiroshige Seko; and the head of the Japanese Business Federation, Sadayuki Sakakibara. *Japan News* commented that Abe has committed himself to an improvement in relations with China through Nikai's participation in the summit.

But even within Europe and in many European Union (EU) member states, the epochal significance of the Silk Road initiative is actually better understood than in Berlin. Czech President Milos Zeman will be the only EU head of state participating in the Beijing summit; former Czech Foreign Minister Jan Kohout commented that the New Silk Road project is a "commercial and political high-speed train toward China, which represents an opportunity for the coming decades." Switzerland, which is not an EU member state, will be represented by its President, Doris Leuthard, just as all of Switzerland is preparing to become a hub for the Belt and Road. Five more EU countries are sending their prime ministers, among them Italy's Paolo Gentiloni and Spain's Mariano Rajoy. The remaining EU members either won't participate or are sending ministers, such as, for example, German Economics Minister Brigitte Zypries.

Unlike in Germany, representatives of Spain, Portugal, Hungary, Serbia, and Greece have expressed enthusiasm about the potential that the New Silk Road opens up for their countries. Spain's ambassador to China, Manuel Valencia, praised the successful collaboration between Spanish infrastructure companies and Chinese companies in the widening of the Panama Canal, the fast train between Mecca and Medina (Saudi Arabia), and the construction of the largest refinery in Kuwait. He said the Canary Islands would be a "peaceful aircraft carrier for enterprise and trade," and that Spain was predestined to be the link between Europe and Asia.

Portuguese Economics Minister Manuel Caldeira Cabral proposed, at the first Sino-Portuguese Economic Forum, that Portugal fully align itself with the Belt and Road Initiative, whose strategy it fully shares. Portugal sees itself as a pivotal country that could be a bridge between Europe and Asia, as an entry point into Europe. Hungarian Foreign Minister Peter Szijjarto stressed that world politics and the world economy are at a point of profound change, and that China's role is not only important for its own future, but also decisive for the future of Europe, which could only profit from the Belt and Road initiative. The list of such declarations could be extended to include those of representatives of several other nations.

Then consider that, despite the U.S. bombing of the Syrian air force base, the relationship between Presidents Trump and Putin, and between Foreign Minister Lavrov and Secretary of State Tillerson, has again become one of cooperation. This is expressed, for example, in the agreement on de-escalation zones in Syria and the dispatch of a U.S. Deputy Secretary of State to the Syria negotiations in Astana, Kazakhstan. This makes clear that an opportunity for collaboration between the United States, Russia, and China is emerging, a collaboration which is obviously crucial for establishing world peace and resolving many flashpoints.

In contrast, Chancellor Merkel's policy positions were very negative—such as those she expressed in her Moscow visit with Putin in her appraisal of the Ukraine crisis, or her maintenance of sanctions, or the brutal austerity policy of the EU and her Finance Minister Schäuble against Greece. The German government has a very reserved attitude toward the New Silk Road—an attitude in complete contrast to the interests of the economy and the well-being of the people. It is probably an expression of the fact that those in Berlin and Brussels do not want to break from the geopolitical outlook that dictates that the EU, as a regional superpower with global ambitions, must defend itself against China, Russia, and the United States.

In early May, Xinhua wrote that it would obviously not be easy for the West, which holds competition in high esteem, to understand the Chinese outlook, which is based on harmony and stability. It said that China is not seeking a global leading role through the Silk Road Initiative, but that the Initiative is in response to the 2008 financial crisis, from which the world economy is still struggling to recover. However, Xinhua pointed out, the Initiative is not an elite club for the western nations, but primarily serves the developing countries. It is a circle of friends, with representatives of more than a hundred nations, and the western nations should be more receptive to the Belt and Road.

To express the point less diplomatically: Nations that cling to geopolitics and close their minds to the new paradigm of win-win cooperation, risk appearing before history as an obstacle to the only strategic initiative that can offer the solution for the urgent problems of mankind, and which is poised on the brink of success.

Let Our Victories of the Past Inform Our Shared Success in the Future!

by Michael Steger

A statement for the Immortal Regiment march in remembrance of those who fought and gave their lives in World War II.

May 6—The Soviet losses during World War II are unimaginable to most Americans, a staggering loss of some thirty million lives, not to mention the destruction of families, industry, land, culture, and infrastructure. Only the Chinese, who lost some twenty million during the fight with Japan, can possibly fathom the kind of sacrifice the Soviet peoples endured, such as the siege of Leningrad, before they prevailed. Such fortitude, such perseverance and courage, are a testament to the power of humanity against a force of evil dedicated to the destruction not only of human lives, but of mankind's unbounded future.

It is this power of humanity, seen in the Soviet resistance and the eventual Allied victory that we celebrate today, and also in those individuals from every nation who bore that burden with dignity and an undying passion for the future of mankind.

Where Do We Go From Here?

The collaboration between the three great powers: the U.S.A., the Soviet forces, and China, was key to the allied victory in World War II, and remains the cornerstone for a new world system today.

President Franklin Roosevelt, who recognized the role of the Soviet Union under Josef Stalin, as well as the efforts of both the Nationalist and Communist Chinese against Japan, personally rejected any attempt to maintain the British Empire's policy of colonization or conflict, and looked to a world of collaboration between the emerging independent nations of the world, especially including Soviet Russia, China, and India.

FDR's post-war view was entirely different than the one implemented by Britain's Churchill and President Harry Truman after FDR's death. But, following the war in the Pacific, an artificial separation was made by British imperial and Wall Street interests, specifically to divide these three major nations into Cold War enemies.

It is now time for the legacy of the Cold War to end. As U.S. Secretary of State Rex Tillerson said to members

EIRNS/Lena Platt

Photos from the Immortal Regiment march in West Hollywood, California, on May 7.

of the U.S. State Department on May 3, 2017:

"The way we have been delivering our mission was in many ways shaped and as a residual of the Cold War era. And in many respects, we've not yet transitioned ourselves to this new reality… and you can see when we have our conversations with NATO—another example—there are many institutions around the world that were created during a different era.

"So one of the things, as we get into this opportunity to look at how we get our work done, is to think about the world as it is today and to leave behind—well, we do it this way because we've been doing it this way for the last 30 years or 40 years or 50 years, because all of that was created in a different environment.

"I guess what I'm inviting all of you to do is to approach this effort that we're going to undertake with no constraints to your thinking—with none."

EIRNS/Lena Platt

Photos from the Immortal Regiment march in West Hollywood, California, on May 7.

U.S.-Russia-China Alliance for Development on the One Belt One Road

The ongoing attacks against the new U.S. Presidency are aimed specifically at maintaining this Cold War divide, even at the cost of the dangers of nuclear war. Yet the Trump Presidency, as we see with Tillerson's comments above, presents a unique opportunity to finally fulfill the potential which was created with the Allied victory in what is called in Russia the Great Patriotic War, and unite these three great nations towards what President Xi of China describes as a "community of common destiny."

The Putin-Xi-Trump alliance is the cornerstone for a new world system, an alliance which can both resolve the remaining geopolitical hot spots left over by Obama's British imperial provocations—such as Syria, Ukraine, and North Korea—and initiate a new global development program based on China's One Belt One Road initiative. The OBOR, initiated just a little over three years ago, is already twelve times the size of the Marshall Plan during its time, and already extends from East Asia to East Africa, from the Indian Ocean to Russia, and as far west as Portugal and the British Isles.

With the U.S., Russia, and China working to develop the interconnections of nations throughout Eurasia, Africa, and into the Americas via the Bering Strait, it is possible to establish both a durable peace among the great powers based on the common aims of man-

EIRNS/Lena Platt

kind, as well as the necessary reconstruction and development of the U.S. after decades of economic destruction, financial speculation, and war.

So, for all of us who honor our loved ones, those who sacrificed everything so that we may celebrate their victory today, what better way to honor them than finally to fulfill the great potential their undying legacy created.

For those veterans still living, such as Lyndon LaRouche, who has personally fought to fulfill FDR's vision ever since returning from his post in Burma, and for the many who have already passed, the alliance of the U.S., Russia, and China, with the aim of global development, gives ultimate meaning to their sacrifices.

EIR Contents

www.larouchepub.com Volume 44, Number 19, May 12, 2017

Xinhua

Cover This Week

The first Silk Road freight train from Xi'an arrives in Budapest, April 22, 2017.

RAISING MANKIND'S STANDARD: THE EURASIAN LAND-BRIDGE

EDITORIALS

2 The New Silk Road Opens a New Perspective for Mankind
by Helga Zepp-LaRouche

5 Let Our Victories of the Past Inform Our Shared Success in the Future!
by Michael Steger

I. SOCIETY AND ECONOMY

8 HELGA ZEPP-LAROUCHE
The Future of the Americas Lies in the New Silk Road

17 'Win Win' Agriculture Can End the Era of Food Warfare, Famine
by Marcia Merry Baker

25 LAROUCHE IN 1992 ON FOOD AND AGRICULTURE
What Would America's Family Farms Look Like in an Economic Recovery

27 How To Tell the Future
by Lyndon H. LaRouche, Jr.

II. BEYOND THE LIES ABOUT THE UNITED STATES

47 Give Economic Development a Chance
by Rachel Brown

49 INTERVIEW: William Binney
'We Are Watching Our Democracy Go Down the Drain'

EDITORIALS

56 Our Mission to Future Mankind
by Diane Sare

59 On the Occasion of the 50th Anniversary of the Belt and Road Summit—2067
by Kesha Rogers

I. Society and Economy

HELGA ZEPP-LAROUCHE

The Future of the Americas Lies in the New Silk Road

This is Helga Zepp-LaRouche's prerecorded keynote address to a May 4, 2017 conference on the theme, "The Future of Ibero-America Lies in the New Silk Road," which was broadcast to meetings gathered in Mexico City, Hermosillo, and Querétaro (Mexico); Lima and Pucallpa (Peru); and Guatemala City (Guatemala). It was also streamed live over the Internet.

Dear Friends of the Schiller Institute,

I will speak to you on the theme, "The Future of Ibero-America Lies in the New Silk Road." I send my most heartfelt greetings to you who are watching the video in Peru, Guatemala, Mexico, Argentina, Chile, Colombia, the Dominican Republic, the United States, and maybe elsewhere.

We are only days away from an event that will make clear to the whole world that the world *is* changing, that we are already in the process of developing a completely new paradigm, that of the New Silk Road, otherwise called the Belt and Road Initiative. In Beijing, between the 14th and 15th of May, a summit will take place. Already 28 heads of state and government leaders have agreed to attend, and the heads of state include those of Argentina and Chile, but also there will be high-level representatives and delegates from 110 nations, altogether 1,200 delegates; there will be 60 international organizations represented. And in the context of this summit, China and 20 countries will sign a cooperation agreement that will define the goals and principles; it will develop an new international platform for

Schiller Institute

Helga Zepp-LaRouche

science and technology, for exchanges and training of talent among the participating countries.

This Belt and Road Forum will be an historic event. It will be the consolidation of a process which started three years and eight months ago, when President Xi Jinping in Kazakhstan announced the New Silk Road. And in this period, the true conception of "win-win cooperation" among altogether almost 70 nations, has become a reality, where it is clear that no longer is this a zero-sum game in which one gains an advantage at the expense of the other, but rather, this is a true "win-win cooperation," in which each country is to have equal benefits from such cooperation.

The significance of this conception of the Belt and Road Initiative lies in this, that for the first time in human history, it overcomes geopolitics—which was the cause of two world wars in the Twentieth Century—because it establishes a higher level of reason, and since it is open to every country, it can reach into the farthest corners of the world. It is open to all nations of the world, including the United States and the European nations, even though they are still not so clearly in favor of it, or at least it's a mixed situation.

Since this program has been put on the agenda by Xi Jinping, it has led to an unbelievable explosion of development, absolutely unprecedented in history. China has signed more than 130 bilateral and regional transport agreements. It has opened 356 international road routes, for both passengers and freight; there are now

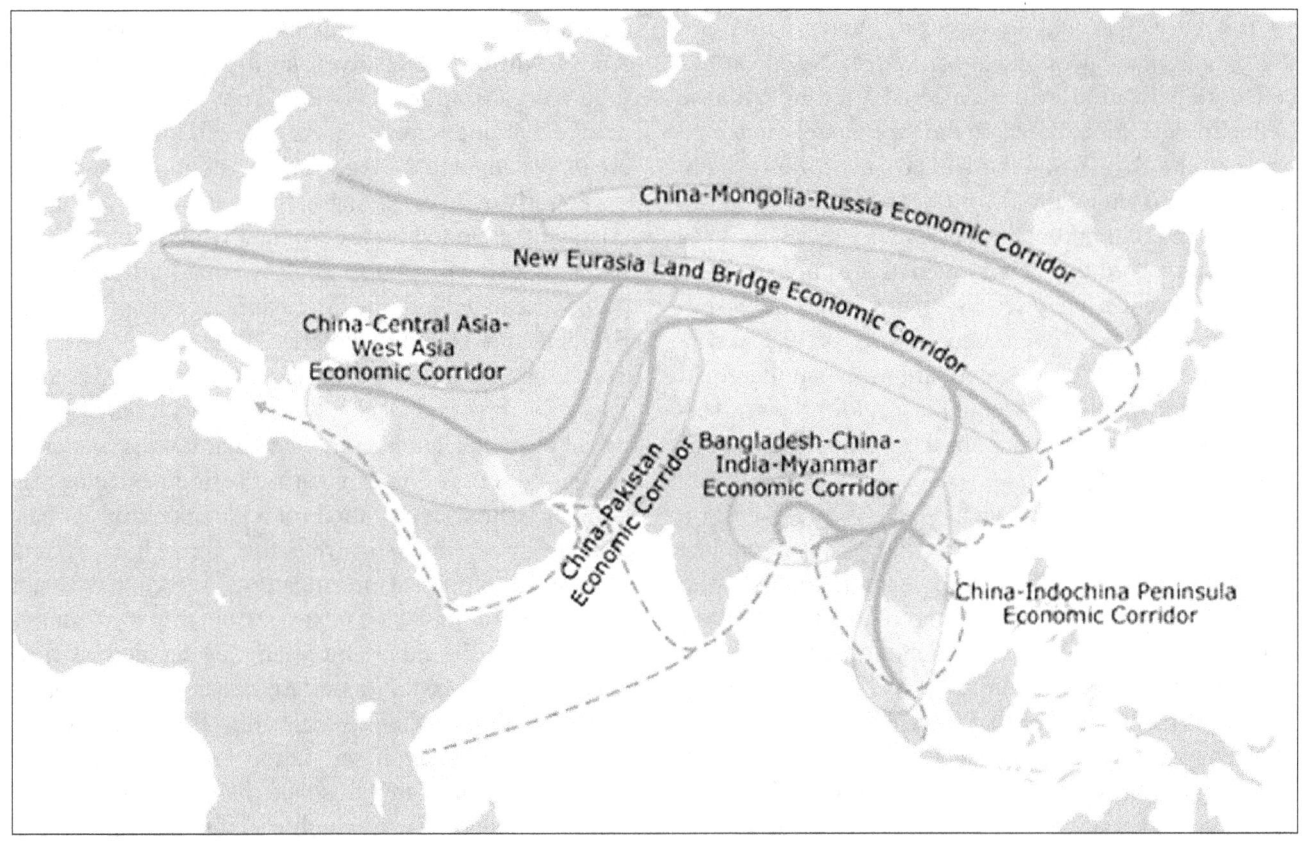

The Belt and Road Initiative: six economic corridors spanning Asia, Europe and Africa.

4,200 direct flights connecting China with 43 Belt and Road countries; there are now 39 China-Europe freight train routes; there is now a cargo train departing Chongqing daily for a European destination.

Meanwhile there are six major industrial development corridors and the 21st Century Maritime Silk Road. The six are:

1. The corridor from China to Central and Western Asia, intended to be extended through Iraq, Syria, Turkey, and into Europe and Africa

2. A corridor from China to Western Europe, which goes from such cities as Chengdu, Chongqing, Yiwu, and Lianyungang to Duisburg, Hamburg, Rotterdam, Lyon, and Madrid

3. The Mongolia-China-Russia corridor, which involves 32 large projects

4. The China-Pakistan Economic Corridor (CPEC), in which China has invested $46 billion and this project is creating 700,000 new jobs in Pakistan

5. The Bangladesh-China-India-Myanmar (BCIM) corridor bridging the Southeast Asia region

6. The China-Indochina Peninsular Corridor

And, there is also the development of an entire railway network in Eastern and Central Africa.

This is unprecedented in human history. After literally centuries of suffering colonialism and poverty and underdevelopment, for the very first time, through this Chinese initiative, there is the prospect for the developing countries to overcome poverty, hunger, and underdevelopment, and to realize their true potential.

Elites in Denial

Well, it is most astounding. But then, it is not so astounding—if you think about it—that there is almost nothing being reported in the mainstream media about this greatest infrastructure project in all history, at least not in the United States and Western Europe. *Forbes* magazine is one of the very few exceptions: It had a six-part series about the potential of the New Silk Road. All of the other mainstream media pretend it doesn't exist. So the populations of Europe and the United States know very little about it, and once they realize it, mainly through our efforts—the efforts of the Schiller Institute—they realize that this is a tremendous potential also for *their* future. For the most part, people get extremely angry that they have been deprived of this knowledge.

It is very clear that the forces of the old paradigm, the paradigm of geopolitics—a system based on so-called globalization, which emerged after the collapse of the Soviet Union, based on the "special relationship" between the British and the United States, this system which was based on profit for the rich, making the gap between the rich and poor ever wider—these old geo-politicians regard this new system as a complete threat to their existence. They see a system which is now specifically aiming to overcome poverty in the whole world and have a "win-win" relationship among equal nations with equal rights, equal respect for their sovereignty. So they try to maintain the illusion that it does not exist.

A very interesting article, "The Existential Question of Whom to Trust," by Robert Parry, appeared just today. Parry is a U.S. investigative journalist who became rather famous through his coverage of the Iran-Contra affair. He writes, "The looming threat of World War III, a potential extermination event for the human species, is made more likely because the world's public can't count on supposedly objective experts to ascertain and evaluate facts. Instead, careerism is the order of the day among journalists, intelligence analysts, and inter-national monitors—meaning that almost no one who might normally be relied on to tell the truth can be trusted." He says—and I fully agree—that what re-places objective reporting is "groupthink," where ex-perts "have sold themselves to … powerful interests in order to keep high-paying jobs and … don't even seem to recognize how far they've drifted from principled professionalism."

Well, that will not help them, because the positive alternative of the Belt and Road Initiative does exist, and it is also the remedy to the two existential crises facing human civilization at this point: First, the danger of a global nuclear war, which is now most obvious in the crisis around the two Koreas, and naturally, still to a certain extent the situation in Syria; and secondly, the danger of an uncontrolled economic crash possibly to occur this year, which if it were to occur would lead to uncontrollable chaos, out of which the danger of a nuclear war would arise as well.

Chaotic Blowout or Glass-Steagall?

Let's briefly look at the second danger. On July 25th, 2007, my husband, Lyndon LaRouche made a truly history forecast: He said, this present global financial system is hopelessly finished, and all you will see

now are the different elements coming to the surface. And it will not be resolved until you have complete, total reorganization of this bankrupt system through a number of measures—Glass-Steagall, a return to a credit system, and the American System of economy.

Exactly one week later, the secondary mortgage crisis in the United States erupted, which then, since it was not dealt with by the measures that LaRouche pro-posed, escalated into the big financial crash of Lehman Brothers and AIG in September 2008.

At that point, for a very short period of time, actually some days and weeks, the leaders of trans-Atlantic world were absolutely convinced that it was a systemic crisis, and some of them, such as President Nicolas Sarkozy of France, even called for a New Bretton Woods, because they were so afraid that the whole system would disintegrate. Unfortunately, this shock did not last very long, and at the next G20 meeting in Washington, on Nov. 15, of the same year, they decided in effect to paper it over, go for quantitative easing, and use other so-called "tools" of the central banks. Rather than going for the Glass-Steagall separation law of Franklin D. Roosevelt, which my husband has prescribed, they went into Dodd-Frank, which was just a cover story to keep the high-risk speculation of the big banks going.

Toward a Chaotic Blowout

In the meantime, the European Central Bank (ECB), the central banks of Great Britain and Japan, and the U.S. Federal Reserve decided to go into quantitative easing, and they created $15 trillion in lending facilities to the too-big-to-fail banks; that has meant a *de facto* zero-interest rate for about ten years. They spent part of this money for so-called bailout packages, which sup-posedly went to countries such as Greece, but in reality 97% of these bailout packages went back to the big Eu-ropean banks and the American banks.

In the United States, this liquidity pumping has in-creased so much that, for example, corporate debt has risen since 2008 from $8 to $14 trillion—that is an in-crease of 75%—of which almost $9 billion is in com-mercial mortgage-backed securities (CMBS). Since 2013, 80% of the corporate borrowing has been used, not for productive investment, but so-called "financial engineering." That is, corporate firms buy up their own stocks to drive up the price, or they're buying other firms in so-called mergers and acquisitions (M&As) for the same effect. They are using $500 billion per year to drive up those stock indexes, while at the same time,

IMF

International Monetary Fund representatives present the Global Financial Stability Report at a press briefing during the IMF's 2017 Spring Meeting.

betting on the derivatives of these manipulations.

Despite all of this, the total non-financial corporate profits have not increased since 2011 and began falling in 2013. Morgan Stanley just put out a report in April that the ratio of non-financial corporate debt to cash from operations is at an all-time high, at a ratio of 3.2 to 1.

With this situation, in which debt is going through the roof relative to the operating cash and profits are declining,— normally, what firms used to do, is go to the banks and borrow more, but this is no longer happening; the banks won't give any more credit because they know this whole system is coming to an end, and it's not maintainable.

Trump Committed to Glass-Steagall

At the April annual meeting of the International Monetary Fund (IMF) in Washington, it put out a 2017 Global Financial Stability Report, in which it wrote that the U.S. debt-service-to-income ratio of the non-financial corporations has gone up 37% in 2014, to 41% in 2016; and those corporations have $7 trillion more debt than in 2008, but $3 trillion less equity invested in them. As a result, a wave of defaults has already started. The default rate for the non-financial corporations jumped from 3% at the beginning of 2016 to 5% at the end, and it is expected to be 5.6% in June. The IMF warns that if interest rates go up, as they did in the period from November to January, then 20% of all U.S. corporations could default. Now that is higher than the highest mortgage default rate in the crash of 2008.

This gigantic bubble of corporate debt is made the more unpayable because of the complete lack of growth in the real economy. The miserable 0.7% growth in GDP, published for the United States—and remember that the GDP statistics are always manipulated, and every knowledgeable person in Europe, for example, makes jokes about it—it went up only 0.7% in the first quarter of this year, and that does not pay for this huge bubble.

But the problem is not only in the United States, it is also in Europe. Just recently, the Italian Banking Association put out the figures of the Level 3 derivatives in the European countries; the highest ratio is in Germany, it was 25.5%; British banks, 25.4%; French banks, 20.5%. And Italy, which is always scolded for having the biggest commercial losses, has only 15%. Now, Level 3 derivatives are derivatives that don't have a market price because nobody wants to buy them; people know they are completely toxic. So they are assets collateralized with debt and therefore pretty worthless, but the ECB has allowed each of the banks to price them according to its own bank model and count them as assets. In the recent stress tests of the European central banks, they left out Level 3 assets, so this is a complete illusion which is being maintained because an admission would basically reveal the complete bankruptcy of the system.

There is only one way to prevent a chaotic blowout, and that is to implement the Glass-Steagall law, which Franklin D. Roosevelt implemented in 1933. There are at present Glass-Steagall bills in both Houses of the U.S. Congress, and the director of the National Economic Council, Gary Cohn, recently told a group of senators that the Trump administration is absolutely committed to realizing Glass-Steagall soon, and that President Trump will fulfill his election promise to go for Glass-Steagall. As a result, there has been a flood of articles in the last three weeks attacking Glass-Steagall, saying it would not have solved the problem of 2008—

which is a complete lie—and obviously, this expresses the complete nervousness of Wall Street and the City of London because it would bankrupt them and cut their power down to size.

A Change in the Wind from China

The situation in China is different. Unlike the asset-based economy of the United States, and partially of Europe, where there is great diversity among the EU members and therefore the whole Eurozone does not function, where basically the situation is completely unsustainable as well, China on the other side, in the first quarter of 2017, had a surprisingly high growth in GDP of 6.9%, compared to the first quarter of 2016. All the agencies—Bloomberg, PricewaterhouseCoopers, and others—agree that the primary driver of this Chinese economic growth is the extraordinary investment in infrastructure, both in China domestically, as well as in the Belt and Road countries.

There was a study of PricewaterhouseCoopers in February that said the great infrastructure projects grew in the last year by 50% in value, and there is a new study by the U.S. National Bureau of Economic Research that says—based on physical economic factors such as the illumination seen by night from space—that the Chinese economy is actually growing faster than even the Chinese government reports.

Chinese factory output is up by 7.6% in the first quarter also, compared to the first quarter of 2016. Household disposable income went up by 7.5%; retail spending up by 10.4%.

Xinhua reported that the goods trade between China and the Belt and Road countries went up by 26.2% in the first quarter. Chinese exports to Belt and Road countries went up by 15.8% in the first three months. Imports to China went up by 42.9% from the 60 countries of the Belt and Road. There are 781 new companies with investments in the Belt and Road countries. Chinese enterprises signed 952 contracts in 61 countries along the Belt and Road.

The Chinese economy and the Belt and Road Initiative has long since become the real engine of the world economy.

So for the United States to come out its present financial danger, there is only one way out, and that is to implement the Four Laws of Lyndon LaRouche: First, Glass-Steagall. Separate the commercial and the investment banks, write off the unpayable debt and toxic paper of the investment banks, put the commercial banks under protection. Then, go to a credit system in the tradition of Alexander Hamilton, implement a National Bank, and increase the productivity of the economy by making a massive investment in fusion technology and space cooperation, and other vanguard technologies to increase the productivity of the labor force.

This could be massively helped by the Chinese cooperating with America on the Belt and Road Initiative, which was offered by President Xi Jinping at the recent Florida summit of Presidents Trump and Xi.

Trump has said he wants to invest $1 trillion in infrastructure in the United States. The American Society of Civil Engineers estimates that the real need for infrastructure investment is $4.5 trillion, but Chinese experts estimate that what the United States really would need is $8 trillion. And China could easily help America to rebuild its infrastructure because it has extraordinary expertise from having done the Belt and Road project for the last three and a half years. China also has already offered to invest its $1.4 trillion they're holding in U.S. Treasury bonds. If this were to be channeled, let's say, through either an infrastructure bank in the United States or a National Bank in the tradition of Hamilton, this could help to revive the American economy.

Now, the same goes for European nations: They urgently need Chinese investment, because the EU has not been providing it, and that is why right now, you have the complete turning around of European nations—they want to be part of the New Silk Road. Greece, Serbia, Hungary, the Czech Republic, Belarus, but also Italy and Portugal, have all stated that they want to become "hubs" of the New Silk Road. So there is a complete change in the wind, representing the potential to realize this fantastic new perspective.

Nuclear War Threat: the Koreas

However, the second existential crisis, the danger of nuclear war, is obviously centered right now very massively around the North Korea crisis. Again, there, the solution will be the integration of the two Koreas into the New Silk Road. But the situation is now extremely dangerous. Pope Francis just put out a statement saying, "the situation has become too hot," that the world is at the brink of war, and he said, "We are talking about the future of humanity. Today, a widespread war would destroy—I would not say half of humanity—but a good part of humanity, and of culture, everything, everything. It would be terrible. I don't think that humanity today would be able to withstand it."

North-South Korea Rail Connections.

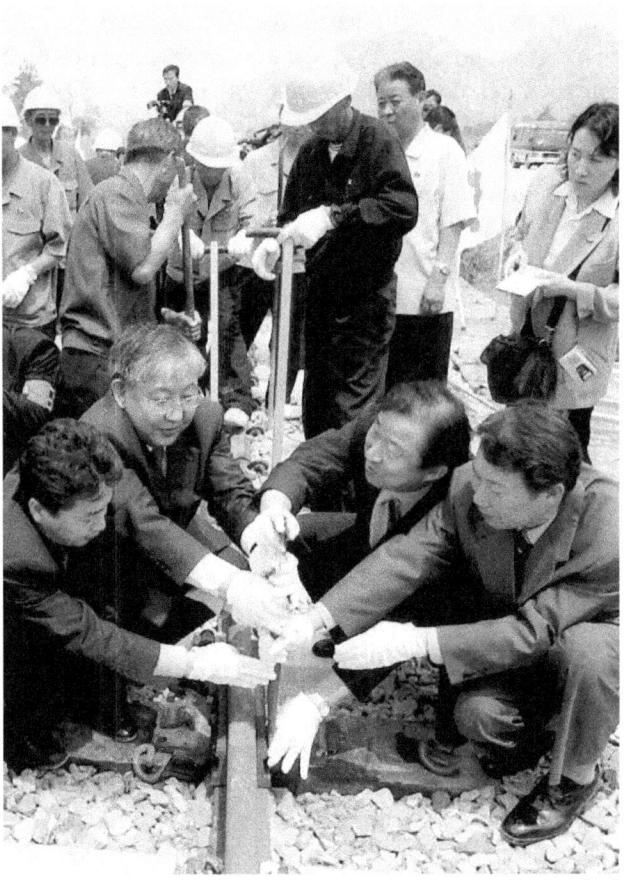

June 15, 2003 ceremony linking North and South Korea rail lines.

If you study the logic of thermonuclear war, the danger is not half of humanity, the danger is that it could lead to the extermination of all life, of all human life on this planet.

This danger is the result of the old geopolitical manipulation, because the situation in Korea is not insoluble at all. In the 1990s and again in 2002, we were very close to establishing a permanent peace on the Korean Peninsula. North Korea, at that time, in the 1990s, had signed the Nuclear Nonproliferation Treaty (NPT); it agreed not to build a nuclear weapons plant, and in return it was allowed to build a peaceful nuclear energy facility. Then at a certain point, U.S. Defense Secretary William Perry in the Clinton Administration was convinced that Pyongyang was diverting plutonium, and he was actively considering the option to take out the North Korean Yongbyon plant in a surgical strike.

At that point, former President Jimmy Carter went to Pyongyang and met with North Korean leader Kim Il-sung, and they reached an agreement which was supported by the Clinton administration, South Korea, and North Korea, with the support of China, Japan, and Russia, and they called this the Agreed Framework, which included the idea that North Korea would take down its Yongbyon plant in exchange for which the United States would help North Korea build a full-scale 1,000 MW nuclear plant and would also provide North Korea with oil until this plant was ready. Inspectors from the International Atomic Energy Agency (IAEA) went there and started to monitor, and there were

pledges that they would move very quickly towards a peace agreement surpassing the armistice which still existed—and still exists.

But then, unfortunately, the Clinton administration came to its end, and was replaced by the Bush and Cheney administration, which immediately started this talk which we know only too well from more recent days, that they couldn't cooperate with a "brutal dictator." That put a cloud over the whole project. But still, in 2002, South Korean President Kim Dae-jung adopted the "Iron Silk Road" proposal, initially proposed by Lyndon LaRouche, who had always maintained that the way to solve the Korea crisis is with the New Silk Road, that you have to build the railroad from Busan at the southern tip of South Korea, through North Korea, all the way to Rotterdam. And that once you have South Korean and North Korean engineers working together building railways, the real basis for peace could be established.

So work on the two railroads began, with a line going from Seoul, via Kaesong in the south of North

Korea, to the old Silk Road, the Chinese railway. And one was supposed to go up the east coast to North Korea and then link up in Vladivostok with the Trans-Siberian Railroad. Also in 2002, in the village of Kaesong, the two governments started to build an industrial park, where South Korean companies deployed very highly skilled North Korean labor to set up factories and build up industries, and things actually went along very well. Meanwhile, there were Six-Party Talks supporting this Sunshine Policy of the South Korean President.

At the time, Bush and Cheney reluctantly went along with it, but always kept nagging North Korea as cheating, saying "don't believe them," and so on. At a certain point, the Six-Party Talks ended, and when Obama came in, and started his "Asia pivot" policy—which was not aimed at North Korea, but really aimed to isolate China and encircle it—they started to build up military forces aimed against China.

Nuclear War or Greater Tumen Initiative

So under pressure from President Obama very recently, South Korean President Park Geun-hye cancelled the Kaesong industrial park and agreed to the deployment of the Terminal High Altitude Area Defense (THAAD) missiles; again, these missiles are not deployed against North Korea, but aimed at China and Russia. Because the North Korean border is only 30 miles from Seoul, North Korea would not need to send ICBMs into space to hit Seoul; North Korea has sufficient artillery for that. But the THAAD missiles have X-band radar, which can see deeply into the territory of China and Russia, which is why both countries have identified the THAAD missiles as an existential threat to their national security.

This is a very dangerous situation. Were North Korea to strike Seoul, all of North Korea would be wiped out in return, the entire North Korean leadership would be killed (as has been stated by many U.S. sources), and the population of Seoul would most definitely also be wiped out. If this war were to escalate, it would clearly have the potential to escalate to Japan and the United States, and it could also lead to a global thermonuclear war.

Right now that danger is absolutely real. The only sign of hope is the positive relationship between Presidents Trump and Xi. At their April 6-7 summit in Mar-a-Lago, Florida, a very positive working relationship and almost friendship developed between the two Presidents. The summit has been called by the Chinese a "complete success." Secretary of State Tillerson has said it has absolutely enhanced mutual trust and both sides have stated that their common aim is the de-nuclearization of Korea, that they want to resolve the conflict through peaceful dialogue.

Now that also requires the implementation of the recent Chinese proposal for a so-called "double suspension"—meaning a suspension of the missiles and nuclear tests on the side of North Korea, and a suspension of the joint military drills on the side of South Korea and the United States. Russia has stated that it completely supports this Chinese policy of double suspension. That would be the first step.

What is needed then, is a comprehensive approach of the New Paradigm, of "double suspension," to include North Korea in the Belt and Road Initiative and integrate the Sunshine Policy with the New Silk Road. The key to it is the collaboration between Xi Jinping and Trump. It can absolutely work, because there are elections on May 9th in South Korea, in which the likely winner has already come out against the THAAD deployment; so the hurried deployment now makes absolutely no sense. And, in the past month, the relationship between Prime Minister Shinzo Abe of Japan and President Putin of Russia has developed in a positive direction, so that you have joint Russian-Japanese investments in the Russian Far East. Therefore, the elements of a solution are absolutely there.

What has to be put on the agenda, therefore, is the Greater Tumen Initiative, which we included in the World Land-Bridge report. This is a regional development project centered on the Tumen River, which forms part of the border between China, North Korea, and Russia. The project would build up the Greater Tumen River Region, including not only China, North Korea, and Russia, but also Mongolia and South Korea, and develop the entire region around it. North Korea was a part of this project until 1993, at least in its initial forms.

The Future of Latin America

So, what has all of this to do with the future of Latin America, and why does my speech have the title, "The Future of Latin America Lies in the New Silk Road"?

I have personally believed for a very long time that the great German mind, the philosopher, statesman, and natural scientist Nicholas of Cusa, in the Fifteenth Century, was absolutely right when he said that the solution to fundamental problems cannot lie in partial remedies, but that you have to find the solution at a higher level of

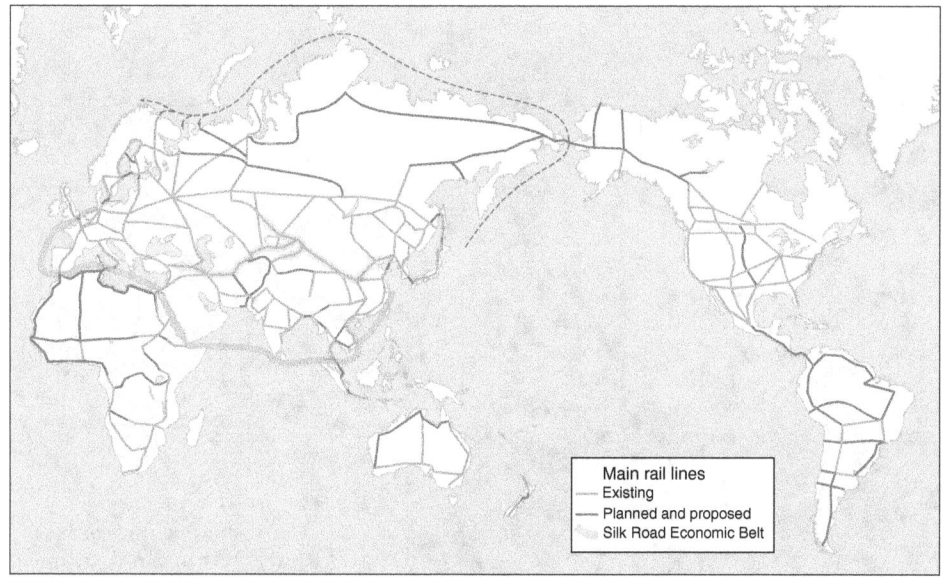

The World Land-Bridge and Maritime Silk Road.

reason, which he called the "coincidence of opposites" or the *coincidentia oppositorum*. You have to establish a level of reason in which the One has a higher reality than the Many, and that is exactly the "win-win cooperation" of the Belt and Road Initiative today.

In the age of nuclear weapons, of the Internet, of air travel, which can bring you in a few hours to any part of the globe, the world has become a very small place. And unlike in previous periods, in which you had one culture going under and some other culture in some other part of the world didn't even know about it, because it would take years to travel from one region to the next, at this time, we are sitting in one boat, and therefore, people have to start to think strategically and not think that the financial crisis of the trans-Atlantic sector—or the North Korea crisis—is something alien to them, but that we have to solve all of these problems simultaneously, or else there will be no solution for anybody.

The only way for Latin American countries to solve the problem of the drug epidemic which is haunting some countries in an existential way, or of poverty, or of underdevelopment, is to revive the development plan of Lyndon LaRouche, which he called in 1982 *Operation Juárez*, when he worked with President José López Portillo to integrate all of Latin America into a single, large infrastructure network. It can be realized today, and it is possible because of the Chinese Belt and Road Initiative.

We have to build a fast train system from the southern tip of Latin America, in Chile and Argentina, going all the way up through Central America and North America to the tip of Alaska, connecting with Siberia through the Bering Strait Tunnel, and in that way linking the trans-American transport corridor with the trans-European-Eurasian infrastructure network.

The infrastructure offered by China is already going in this direction. China has offered financing and other help in the construction of the Bi-Oceanic Railroad, as you will hear in the next presentation—a railroad between Brazil and Peru, and between Brazil and Bolivia.

China is already building a science city in Ecuador. During the recent state visit of President Xi to Ecuador, Peru, and Chile last fall, Xi met with the former President of Ecuador, Rafael Correa, and the two leaders stated their intention that very soon China and Ecuador will both be on the top rung of science and technology, reflecting the state of the art. This is a very ambitious and very hopeful intention.

That Chilean President Michelle Bachelet will go to the Belt and Road Forum in Beijing and then remain for a state visit, represents the potential of bringing all of these projects a big step forward. Chile's former ambassador to China, Fernando Reyes Matta, says that the world leaders who are attending the Belt and Road Forum are betting on the future. He said: Should we think, from Latin America, about linking with the One Belt and Road if it will have the same effect as the Marshall Plan had on Europe? Well, the answer is obviously, yes, because the Belt and Road Initiative is already twelve times larger than the Marshall Plan was in its time, and it is open ended and can be extended without limit.

Toward a Culture of Genius

This fantastic economic development perspective also has—and must have—a cultural dimension. Bolivia, Mexico, and Peru are among the ten member states—all countries with very old cultures—of the Ancient Civilizations Forum, and they sent their foreign ministers to its first ministerial conference in Greece on April 24. These are countries with very proud, ancient traditions that they intend to revive and connect to their ambitions for the future. For the New Silk Road/World

Top left: The Chinese company COSCO is upgrading Piraeus into the largest port in the Mediterranean.

Above: High-speed railway construction in Turkey.

Left: A bullet train running on the Shanghai-Kunming high-speed railway in southwest China's Guizhou Province.

Below: Chinese-built modern railway under construction in Kenya.

Land-Bridge project to succeed, we must revive the best traditions of each nation, of each culture on this planet, and then maintain a dialogue, so that each nation knows about and finds out about the treasures that universal history has so far accomplished.

If we have win-win economic cooperation, it will uplift every human being from poverty, it will unleash the tremendous potential of human creativity, and it will lead—I am absolutely certain—to a new cultural renaissance.

The people of Latin America must absolutely know that we—the human species as a whole—are close to a decisive branching point in human history—that the New Silk Road allows for a completely New Paradigm.

Under the New Paradigm, for example, we will be rid of the old idea of money—the idea that you earn virtual money, and the money figures could disappear from your bank account instantly in a financial crash. That's the idea that what you never really owned, because it was always virtual, you could also never lose.

This wrong idea will be replaced by the concept of a meaningful life in which each person can unfold the fullness of his or her creative potential, something that so far has only been possible for a very few individuals—such geniuses as Dante, Kepler, Schiller, Beethoven, Vernadsky, Einstein. Very few people could reach that level of creativity. Up until now, most people have been so burdened by what they had to do to earn their livelihood, by the constraints of managing their daily lives, that they could not fulfill their potential.

Now it will be possible to change this, and we will have a society, increasingly, on our planet, in which more and more people—and eventually *all* people— can be truly human by developing all of their inherent potentials.

So, provided we can solve the two existential crises that I mentioned, we are looking at a very bright future. If Latin America links up with the Belt and Road Initiative, this potential can be realized for all of us in a very short time.

'Win Win' Agriculture Can End The Era of Food Warfare, Famine

by Marcia Merry Baker

May 7—The images associated with the May 14-15 "Belt and Road Forum for International Collaboration" in Beijing which come to mind first, are the spectacular new transportation and power infrastructure projects—trains, ports, nuclear plants—coming into being at points across nearly 70 participating nations, which are now conferring on how to further the "Silk Road" process, originally announced in September 2013 by Chinese Pres. Xi Jinping.

But equally spectacular, is the prospect of applying the "win-win" principle—which Xi has declared as the spirit of the Silk Road—to agriculture. This means we can bring to an end the era of famine, farm trade wars, and especially, food-as-a-weapon. The images of what can happen range from "protected" agriculture in Siberia to fabulous high yields in the Tropics, will result in a well-fed humanity.

To appreciate the reality of this potential, it is necessary to be clear on the destructive axioms of agriculture policy that have been in play over the last 40 years—institutionalized in the WTO (World Trade Organization, 1995), NAFTA (North American Free Trade Organization, 1994) and other trade deals, which account for today's farm vulnerabilities, while millions still go hungry. In short, now is the time—long overdue—to cancel the WTO and the rigged, evil system behind it.

On April 29, President Trump signed an Executive Order, "Addressing Trade Agreement Violations and Abuses," which mandated a review of all U.S. trade relations, meaning the WTO, NAFTA, and other organizations and deals. A report is due in 180 days, which is to identify where remedial action is called for.

The reality is that no "remedies" nor "reforms" can be devised that will make anything better under the premises of these free-trade regimes. They were put into place on the economic side of geopolitics—pushed by the neo-British empire, and done for the benefit of the super-corporations and financial circles associated with Wall Street and the City of London.

Look at NAFTA and what has happened to the food system of Mexico, the United States, and Canada. Wrong from the start, NAFTA has succeeded, in its own terms, in imposing destructive interdependencies in production and trade of basic foods—corn, meat, milk, fruits, and vegetables, all across North America. These patterns will be a challenge to undo, and set right. It will be hard, but not at all impossible. The needed improvements can be carried out, along with upgrading all the world's food supply. We can act now to create to means for providing "our daily bread" for everyone the world over.

'Lose-Lose' Premises of NAFTA/WTO

First, look at the "lose-lose" premises of the free-trade era. The publicly promoted principles of the

The White House

Pres. Donald Trump at a White House Farmers Roundtable, April 25, with Agriculture Secretary Sonny Perdue (on the left).

GATT (U.S. General Agreement on Tariffs and Trade) WTO, NAFTA and variants, are:

• Competition between and among farmers, and nations will bring about sufficient food through the dynamics of supply and demand.

• "Market" forces will determine fair prices, and induce or restrict production.

• National governments must be dis-allowed from interfering into competition, prices, markets, and other aspects of farming and food: All tariffs, domestic farmer supports and other actions are to cease, because they "distort" the "free" markets.

Robert L. Baker

Corn on the ground in February 2017, at an elevator in Brown County, South Dakota, from the 2016 harvest. Spoilage is a threat. With the farm corn price below cost of production, the entire process of orderly marketing and use is disrupted.

• The ultimate goal is a "One World Market" (the GATT slogan leading up to the founding of the WTO).

• Agro-science progress—for seed genetics and other R&D—comes through giving patent control to monopoly interests. Their "intellectual property rights" shall be enforced over and above the rights of farmers and consumers.

These principles have been increasingly forced into practice since approximately 1984, the time of the start-up of the "Uruguay Round" of the GATT talks in Punta del Este, which began the process of removing world agriculture and trade out from under the control of nations, which was called "de-regulation." In 1994, the North American Free Trade Agreement was signed. It was justified on the same grounds. And in 1995, the World Trade Organization came into effect.

The formation of the WTO is exactly what was rejected after World War II. This same process was then considered to be too destructive of national sovereignty. A proposal was made at the 1944 Bretton Wood conference, for an "International Trade Organization," including de-regulated food trade, but it was roundly defeated as an obviously bad idea.

Neo-British Empire

The WTO axioms which served as a basis for agricultural policy during recent decades, has resulted in the increasing consolidation of control and profiteering by the supra-national corporations and financial interests which had originated the free trade era. From seed and fertilizer, to livestock slaughtering, food processing, grain handling and milling, and final grocery distribution, an increasingly smaller set of huge operations has come to dominate food production and trade. (See Box, p.19)

The British Empire provenance refers to the international echelon of corporate and foreign policy control interests, and the City of London and Wall Street outright. This is true, not only of British Commonwealth-based entities, but also includes cartel members headquartered elsewhere, e.g. Cargill, in Minnesota, and Danone in France. Wall Street money funds have come to own key links in the food chain outright, from mega-farms, to food processing, to final distribution.

The intent of this deregulation, control grab, and "monetization" of food by the British imperial crowd, was not merely profiteering, but to prevent the advancement of prosperous nations and a growing population—seen as a threat by the "empire."

Secondly, the WTO deregulation years have brought into being the wild casino of commodity speculation. Today, the turnover of trades of units of bushels of grain at the Chicago Mercantile Exchange for example, far exceeds the volume of physical product nominally associated with the trading contracts. This Spring, hedge fund speculators in wheat contracts went on a "shorting spree" for nine successive weeks, selling far more futures contracts—in the range of several thousands, more than their purchases.

This is insane betting, though it goes under the WTO euphemism of "risk management." Nowadays, American farmers and ranchers, besides their traditional suppliers of seed, chemicals, machinery, fuel, veterinary services and other costs of production, are expected to employ a "market manager," to deal with their futures, puts, calls, and contracts.

This insanity was pushed during the entire GATT/WTO drive for deregulation of "financial services," but it especially gained ground after the 1999 U.S. repeal of its Glass Steagall Act (the 1933 legislation which separated and insured traditional commercial banking, from speculative financial activity). This was further compounded by the 2000 U.S. enactment of the "Commodities Futures Modernization Act," which ushered in anything-goes commodities speculation.

Dump the WTO, NAFTA

As a result of the WTO practices, many features of our domestic and world food system are blatantly "lose-

---

Consolidation of Control in the Food Chain

by Robert L. Baker

May 7—The United States, and most countries—especially in the trans-Atlantic region, have much of their food systems (production, processing, and retail) concentrated in the clutches of a very small number of big international money groups, primarily centered around Wall Street and London-European banks and old money families. Exceptions are China, and most of Russia and India, but the world impact of the cartels is huge.

To begin with, in the United States, a large share of actual food output comes from a very few, large farm operations. In brief, statistically, the United States has 2.2 million farms (defined to include small operators,) with activities on 922 million acres of farmland, giving an average of 425 acres/farm. Of this base, 75% of all U.S. farm production, comes from 10% of the farms. That is, 90% of the farms produce only 25% of U.S. output.

Look at the degree of consolidation in a few categories of food and production, centered on the United States.

Beef: The United States is the world's largest producer and importer, and 4th largest exporter of beef in the world. Five percent of U.S. feedlots produce 85% of all U.S. grain-fed cattle.

Pork: The United States is the world's third largest producer and largest exporter of pork (30% of world pork trade.) Only 1% of U.S. farm operations produce 90% of U.S. pork.

Chickens: The United States is the world's largest chicken producer, and 2nd largest exporter, with 95% of U.S. production accounted for by about 1% of U.S. farmers, who work with 35 vertically-integrated big companies.

Dairy: The United States is the world's largest producer and exporter of cow's milk, with 20 giant dairy entities producing 76% of the total.

Meatpackers: The top four beef, pork and chicken slaughter entities control 85%, 74% and 54%, respectively, of meat processing. Prominent names include: Tyson, JBS, Cargill, Smithfield, Hormel, National Beef, ConAgra, and SYSCO. The two largest—Smithfield and JBS—are foreign-owned.

Corn: The United States is the world's largest producer and exporter of corn, accounting for 30% of 2015 world exports.

Soybeans: The United States is the world's largest producer of soybeans and 2nd largest exporter.

Ethanol: The United States is the largest producer, exporter and importer, in the world. Most U.S. exports go to Brazil, which is the 2nd largest ethanol producer.

Seed Companies: The Big Six control 63% of world sales and 95% of bio-engineered traits. They are in various stages of attempted mergers. (Monsanto, Syngenta, DuPont, Dow AgroSciences, BASF and Bayer).

Chemicals: The Big Six control 76% of agriculture chemicals.

Fertilizer: One company owns 20% of world production.

FIGURE 1

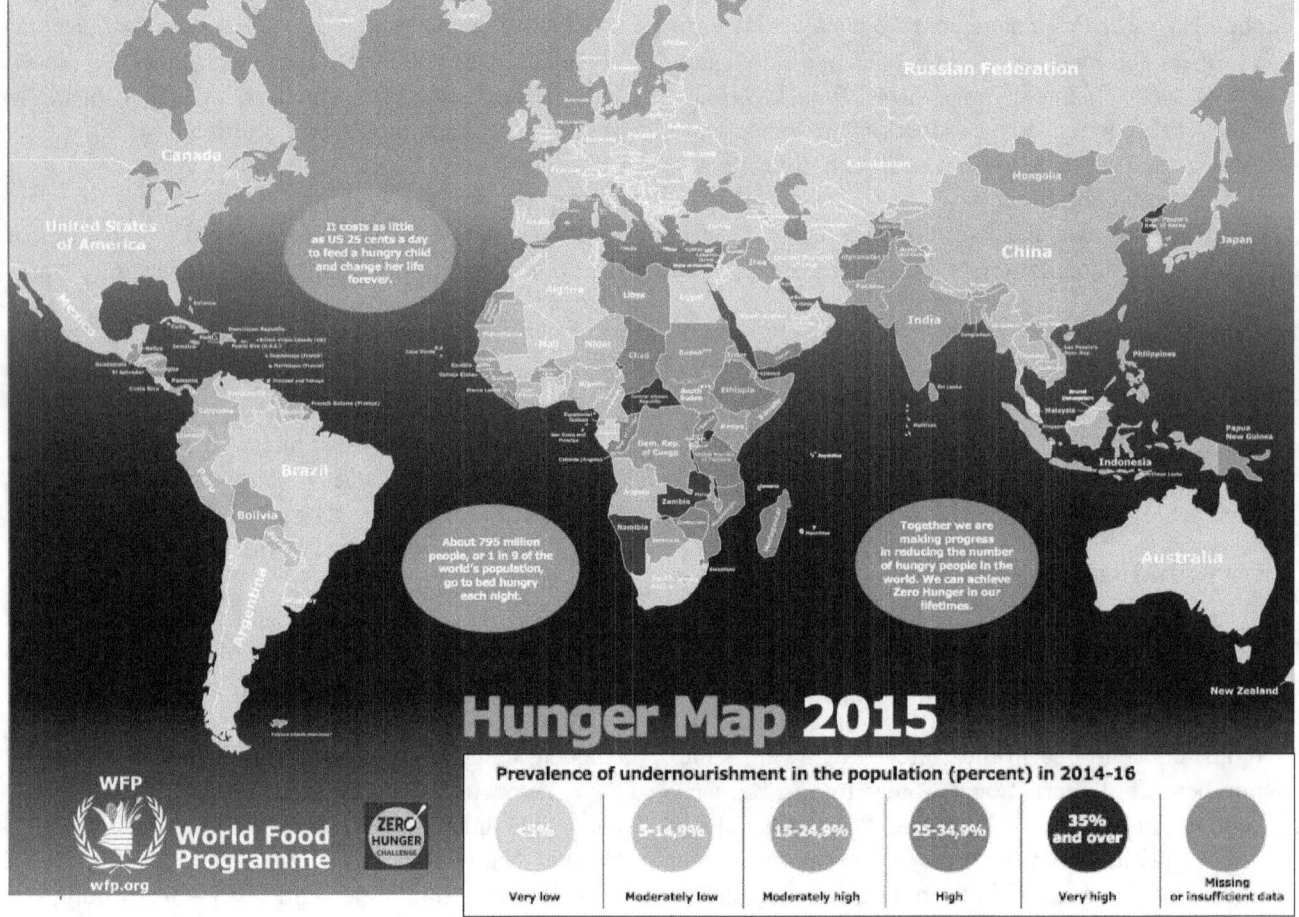

Hunger Map 2015

Prevalence of undernourishment in the population (percent) in 2014-16

<5%	5-14,9%	15-24,9%	25-34,9%	35% and over	
Very low	Moderately low	Moderately high	High	Very high	Missing or insufficient data

lose" for all involved, and must be overturned.

Begin with the fact of world food shortages. **[Figure 1]** shows today's world hunger map. Worldwide, an estimated 795 million people are chronically undernourished, out of our total population of 7 billion. There are many desperate situations. We now have the largest food emergency in Africa (South Sudan, Somalia, Nigeria and elsewhere) since the humanitarian crisis after World War II. The UN estimates that 20 million people could starve. This month, the World Food Program is seeking the means for emergency food for 9 million people in Yemen, for example.

The rough estimate is that for world-wide food sufficiency and security, we should have a goal of producing much more of most necessities as is presently being produced. This is a necessity if we are to provide high-level diets for all cultural preferences, for food reserves, and for supporting output-capacity for the future. As of 2016, some 2.5 billion metric tons of grains (all kinds) are produced yearly. Increasing this (along with tubers), while increasing milk and meat output, as well as more fruits and vegetables, will enable the production of high-level diets for the world's population.

The constraints against sufficient food production and availability are not physical limitations, but the British empire *policy* of deregulation, "free" trade, and promotion of scarcity.

For example, presently, the world commodity prices for milk and certain grains are low—even below the farmers' costs of production—and it is asserted—under WTO logic—that this is the result of a "glut" of food. The WTO logic is that the current low market prices for farm output will eliminate "excessive" food production, and ruin enough farm operations, so that supply will go down, and market prices go back up.

It is against WTO rules for national governments to intervene to provide supports to the farmer (buy-up of output, price controls, floor prices, for example), or

U.S. Average Farm Household Income, On- and Off-Farm Sources Since 1960

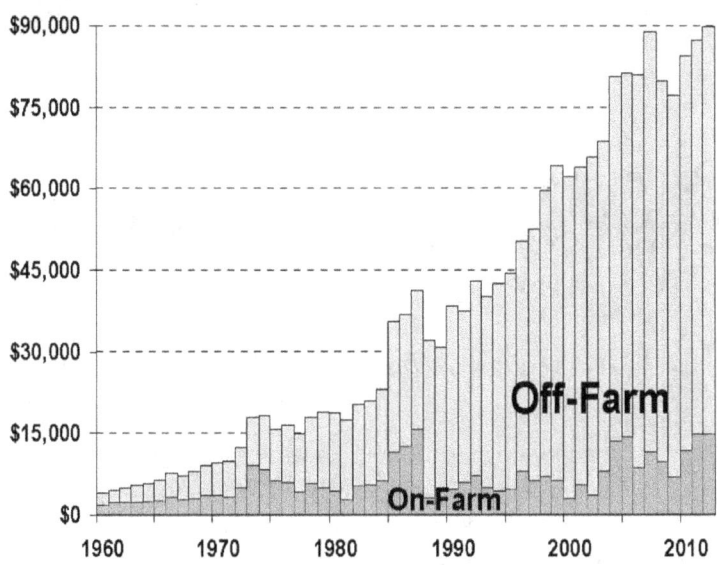

Source: USDA, ERS, "Farm Household Economics and Well-Being: Historic Data On Farm Operator Household Income," November 27, 2012.

The reliance of family farmers on off-farm income, is now even more extreme, since farm commodity prices have been below costs of production from 2013 to the present.

conversely, to induce the farmer to produce more, when there are shortages. This is denounced as "distortion" of markets. Under the Obama Administration, the United States filed a record number of WTO suits against other nations—mostly China—claiming they harmed American farmers by "market distortion."

In fact, under the WTO-exalted "markets" system, U.S. farmers and ranchers are right now suffering bad conditions, without any "distortions" to blame the problem on. The net income of the U.S. farm sector is down 50% from 2013. This is the fourth successive year of farm commodity prices running below what the farmer's cost of production is. Older farmers are quitting. Farm debt is rising. Farmers are even more reliant on off-farm jobs to continue to farm, while losing money. For example, in Iowa, a farmer now might get $3.20 for a bushel of corn, when he has to pay $4.05 to produce it. Under the WTO system, the government may not intervene. Mounds of unsold, unprofitable corn are seen on on the ground in the Cornbelt.

Another destructive characteristic pattern of today's WTO-era food production and trade, is the long-distance cross-hauling of basic commodities, and the worsening of food import- and export-dependence for basic needs. Internationally, there are many examples

of crazy trade flows: for example, green beans from Africa to Europe; peaches from South Africa to the United States; mushrooms from Indonesia, and apple juice concentrate from China to the United States. In WTO-speak, the African and Asian exporting nations are "succeeding" in participating in long-haul food "value chains" to trans-Atlantic nations!

Look at North America in this light. Over the NAFTA/WTO period, two sweeping, destructive patterns were imposed. Mexico was forced to become increasingly dependent on the United States for staples—corn, beans, wheat, while the United States became increasingly dependent on fruits and vegetables (processed and fresh) from Mexico. Otherwise, very complex, cross-border trade takes place in meat and processing, based on cheap labor and other costs.

Annual corn imports into Mexico soared from the level of about 2 million metric tons in the pre-NAFTA early 1990s to over 13 million at present—six times over—coming almost exclusively from the United States. The same trend applies to beans and wheat. In the United States, corn monoculture has taken over much of the farmbelt, especially when the Bush-Obama corn-for-ethanol program went into gear. Today, some 45% of the total U.S. corn harvest goes to ethanol and Mexico. Meantime, in Mexico—where corn originated, the farm sector has been devastated; hunger has spread.

In reverse, Mexico has come to supply a huge share of fruits and vegetables consumed in the United States, most all of which were formerly, easily produced in the United States The NAFTA tariff-free entry into the United States, allowed for trans-Atlantic-based megafood processors and distributors—e.g. Green Giant, Del Monte, Dole, Walmart et al.—to relocate food-sourcing (from onions to tomatoes) by means of imposing conditions of cheap labor, cheap land use, and cheap processing. This undercut Mexico's farm-food system, and put thousands of U.S. family farms and orchards out of business. One example makes the point: over 95% of current U.S. consumption of frozen broccoli comes from Mexico now (with some from Guatemala and Ecuador). Cutting broccoli into florets is labor intensive; production was relocated from California to Mexico under NAFTA.

The obvious must be stressed: none of these food

An ethanol unit train near Aberdeen, South Dakota, in March, 2017. The distillery and corn elevator are seen in the background. Too corrosive for pipelines, ethanol now takes up significant rail transport.

shifts were done to serve the public interests of Mexico or the United States, but instead, the commodities wing of Wall Street/City of London. These very same circles—speaking through corn representatives, and produce-processors and traders, are shrieking that Trump must not dare to change NAFTA.

But the WTO/NAFTA-legacy can be overturned, to the benefit of all the people, not the financial parasites. Nations—their leaders, farmers and experts, can confer on what shifts are desired, what is the timing, the technology and other concerns, and the roll-back of the "free trade" destruction can be made. The principle is to serve the common interest. There are many precedents. One of the most dramatic is World War II, when nation-to-nation collaboration took place for Lend Lease food attangements.

Today, in eastern Siberia, new agriculture projects are underway jointly between Russia and China, with Japanese and other input. In South America, new farm and food development commitments are in place with China, aided by Pres. Xi's visit last November. It is exemplary that China's potato output jumped 40%, after Peru supplied a new potato strain in the 1990s, Much more high technology and agro-science collaboration is planned.

United States-Canada 'Milk War'

Look at the current "milk war" between the United States and Canada, to see how only a "win-win" agriculture policy can work. As of May 1, Canadian cheesemakers ceased buying a specialty dairy product—ultra-filtered milk (proteins concentrate)—from a Wisconsin dairy company, and as of April 1, from a New York firm, which had been, for several years, processing milk sup-

plied by dozens of local farmers in these states for sale in Canada. Suddenly, nearly 60 Wisconsin farmers had no more Canadian market, and in New York state, even more dairymen were caught out.

These deadlines, actually announced months ago, became the occasion in recent weeks for attacks flying back and forth between the United States and Canada, in which claims were made—including by President Trump—that U.S. milk farmers are being unfairly hurt by Canada. Meanwhile, Canada claims its cheesemakers can lawfully switch to using Canadian-produced milk. Trump rightly denounced NAFTA.

How to overcome the conflict—instead of slaughtering milk herds, and suing Canada? Wisconsin and New York officials asked the U.S. Department of Agriculture in early April, to plan to acquire their milk with nowhere to go, and arrange for processing it for storage—milk powder, butter or cheese, as has been done repeatedly since this policy was enacted under Franklin Delano Roosevelt in the 1935 Agriculture Act. The stored milk product can then be used for school or other domestic purposes, or for international food relief, now urgently needed for Yemen and Africa. Meantime, farmers, government officials, and processors can confer on milk supply management, and floor prices on the parity principle. (Box, p. 23)

So far, this hasn't happened. Most of the 58 milk farmers who sold to Canada through Grassland Dairy, Inc., have found other processors to sell to, for at least the next six months. This has saved the herds temporarily, but the farmers' milk price is still below their costs. Dozens of dairy farmers in New York state are desperate. Meantime, the cows must be fed and milked, or killed off.

Shift to Win-Win

There is a strong impetus for a shift. Voters in the U.S. farmbelt, as in the former industrial heartland, voted for Donald Trump massively, for an end to NAFTA and such critical changes as reinstating the Glass Steagall act. Of the 17 states since January, where resolutions have been introduced to tell Congress to restore Glass-Steagall and launch a recovery, many are in farm states, including Iowa, Illinois, Minnesota, Ohio, and Michigan, as well as other states with important farm output—Pennsylvania and New York. President Trump is on record for backing Glass Steagall; he has slammed NAFTA, and ordered a review of the WTO and all trade deals, singling out his commitment to farmers and ranchers.

The collaboration between China and the United States, in the "Silk Road" spirit, can lead the way. In Florida in April, Trump and Xi spoke of restoring U.S. beef exports to China (banned in 2003, over the Mad Cow concern).

There is already a major "soybean connection" between China and the United States. China currently consumes some 100 million metric tons of soybeans a year, and of that amount, over 85 percent is imported, almost entirely from the United States and Brazil.

Outstanding as this soy import-volume is, the dependence on the Americas for soybeans does not go against the commitment of China, in principle, to become food self-sufficient. Rather, the U.S.-China soy connection reflects the reality that China is seeking to provide for an improved diet for 700 million people brought out of poverty in the last 30 years. Twenty years ago, China was importing only some 2 million metric tons (mmt) of soybeans; 10 years ago, China imported 29 mmt. And now the imports are at the 85 mmt level. Among the other win-win U.S. exports to China is pork, a large part of which comes from Iowa. Meantime, China is working on improving domestic agriculture productivity.

The means used in China for rural development and

Prices to U.S. Farmers Are Way Below Parity

The principle of parity-pricing in agriculture was implemented successfully—beginning with the 1933 Agriculture Adjustment Act—through bi-partisan efforts under Franklin Delano Roosevelt and Agriculture Secretary Henry Wallace. Parity pricing provided security for the public food supply, and a surge of output when called for during World War II, and afterward.

The onset of "deregulation" and free markets phased out the parity principle in U.S. farm policy, as of the 1970s. The speculation-serving excuse in its place, is that farmers must engage in "risk management" of their prices—buying, selling, and betting on futures contracts.

Parity refers to the scientifically-calculated pricing system used by the U.S. Department of Agriculture, which mandates a price to the farmer (implemented through various mechanisms) for designated commodities, that will cover produc-

tion costs, including a sufficient amount for providing the level of education and investment to guarantee future generations of high-technology farmers. Parity prices continue to be calculated by the U.S. Department of Agriculture, according to various base years. The following USDA parity statistics—for selected items—are for March, 2017 (USDA, National Agricultural Statistics Service.)

Commodity & Unit	Price Received	Price If 100% of Parity	% of Parity Received
Corn/bushel	$3.50	$13.60	27%
Wheat/bu	4.40	17.60	25
Soybeans/bu	9.75	31.40	31
Beef Cattle per 100 pounds	124.80	320.00	39
Hogs per 100 pounds	53.13	161.00	33
Milk per 100 pounds	18.13	51.80	35
Eggs/dozen	.82	2.94	28
Apples/pound	.35	.98	36
Oranges/box	12.40	25.30	49
Potatoes per 100 pounds	9.10	24.60	37

—Robert L. Baker

reducing poverty include many of the very practices banned by the WTO/NAFTA, e.g. floor prices for farm output, government-purchased food reserves, and non-patented seed development. In fact, these means are essential now for the United States to employ, in collaboration with Mexico and Canada, to phase out the destructive NAFTA farm and food patterns of the last 25 years.

Farmer representatives can specify the measures required, including actions for anti-trust and anti-speculation, fostering of more processing and handling logistics infrastructure, and parity-based floor prices and emergency interventions, especially in perishable farm output like milk. These are the hallmark practices of what came to be called the "American System" in the 1800s, for which Trump has repeatedly announced his support.

One immediate action, is for the United States to dump its WTO damages suit filed against China last year by the Obama Administration, which charges that China's support of its own farmers is causing harm to U.S. farmers! In September 2016, the U.S. anti-China action was filed with the WTO, saying China's price support to its wheat, corn, and rice farmers, serves to encourage them to produce more, which policies "limit opportunities for U.S. farmers to export competitively priced, high-quality grains to customers in China…," as then United States Trade Presentative Michael Froman stated. This is pure British Foreign Office food geopolitics.

Instead, China and the United States can collaborate on using the huge U.S. grains capacity for emergency international food relief, while farm production is upgraded everywhere.

Iowa Gov. Terry Branstad, Trump's appointee for U.S. Ambassador to China, is well positioned to end geopolitical food wars, to further mutually beneficial trade and production measures. Personally, he has a 32-year friendship with Xi Jinping, since Xi first visited Iowa on an agriculture tour in 1985. At present, over 25% of the soy crop of Iowa—a leading producer, goes to China. The state is also a top pork exporter to China, where Branstad visited last Fall, to promote even more

Xinhua/Lan Hongguang

On Feb. 15, 2012 Chinese President Xi Jinping (front, center, then Vice President) appeared with Iowa Gov. Terry Branstad (left of Xi, and now to be U.S. Ambassador to China) at the Mississippi River town of Muscatine, with friends. Xi met Branstad on his first visit to Muscatine in 1985, when Xi toured Iowa farming. The two friends have met many times since.

meat trade.

Branstad spoke at his May 2 Senate Foreign Relations nomination hearing about how trade can be mutually beneficial. Expecting to take up his position by June, Branstad said he will personally visit every province in China.

President Xi has already taken the initiative to put forward what he calls the "framework" of the New Silk Road, as the context for solving world hunger and poverty once and for all. He did this at the United Nations at the time of the September 2016 General Assembly, and again that month at the G-20 meeting in Guangzhou. The UN Development Program endorsed this approach in 2016, and it was ratified by the General Assembly early this year. Now in July in Manhattan, the next opportunity for collaboration on ending hunger comes at the UN meeting of the High Level Political Forum on Sustainable Development at the UN headquarters in New York.

What is the vision for farming in an advancing world? Lyndon LaRouche, who has led the fight against the evil British geopolitics and free trade swindles for decades, often has addressed what agriculture can be. In an article 25 years ago, he speaks of the American System and farming, in terms directly important for today's opportunity.

What Would America's Family Farms Look Like in an Economic Recovery

Below is a transcript of the response on June 15, 1992 by then Demoractic presidential candidate Lyndon La-Rouche to a Food for Peace activist, who asked What America's family farms would look like in an economic recovery which included parity prices and low-interest credit to agriculture?

In talking about a return to an American System farming procedure, we have to look at two things:

One is a resumption of extensive agriculture, that is, essentially, field and related agriculture, combined with an increased emphasis proportionately on modern aeroponics and hydroponics, essentially in high value per pound bush fruits and vegetables. We can economically produce these with a desirable quality of freshness 12 months a year in most areas, within enclosures which are simply hydroponic/aeroponic industrial applications of the same principles with which farmers are familiar, in field agriculture.

By that I mean, in these enclosures, we can do, in general, what we do with the chicken hotel running on chain drive. We can also control the atmosphere variably; we can control growth through aeroponic as well as hydroponic methods; we can do all kinds of things. But essentially, the mental abilities, the skills, required are the same as those of the farmer, plus a few things to which the farmer would have to adapt to run one of these things.

Rebuild the Cities

Since the cities of the United States are in degenerate condition as a result largely of the postwar suburbanite policy and because of the bankruptcy of real estate, we're going to go through a restructuring of both urban and rural life, especially urban life.

In the process, if we are rational—and our planning for space colonization and improved desalination and water management technologies will help to accelerate this process—we will head in the direction of creating green zones around major urban centers.

The green zone would be essentially an area of supply of some meat, which means the return to some slaughter, butchery, to the urban region, locally. I'm thinking of especially meats, and also, high-priced vegetables, that is, high-priced per pound value, into this kind of production. Asparagus, certain cabbages, and all this sort of thing, and certain kinds of bush fruits, such as, for example, raspberries, strawberries, gooseberries, and dwarf tree fruit in those areas.

Agriculture around the cities will have two functions: to create a green zone, which an expanding farm operation is suited to: land management and land maintenance, which is what a farm does automatically if it has parity price. Thus, that change in composition will become more and more the case, with field agriculture used for other things which are of lower value per pound of product, such as potatoes, grains, and other crops.

When we think about all these things, we have to think about the size of land area which a family farm or inter-family farm can manage, so we're talking about the corresponding number of hundreds of hectares, 100 hectares and up generally, even with very efficient land use, is what can be managed, if we include, for example, a certain amount of reserve land. There will be more a tendency to have reserve-maintained farmland, that is, with a proper cover, to improve land not in use.

So essentially, I think, most land of farmland type not in use should be within farms; and under a parity structure, the farmer would be accorded a price, or shall we say, a payment, for maintaining the reserve ratio of land for future use or rotational use, as well as the land actually in production. That would be the best way of handling most of the farm reserve land, that is, to keep it in part of the production cycle under management-ownership. There is a policy of keeping reserve land being farmed under proper cover as an integral part of farming, rather than having it as something separate, in large trustholdings, which is just completely inefficient.

Let me say one other thing about the family farm.

Let's take a comparable issue. Let's take the function of the middle-level high-tech industry in the vertical integration of industry as a whole.

Is it better to have the research laboratories in tool

EIRNS

Lyndon LaRouche addressed the second international Food for Peace Conference in Chicago, December, 1988, on the theme, "Give Us This Day Our Daily Bread." He co-founded the Food for Peace effort of the Schiller Institute earlier that year, with his wife, Helga Zepp-LaRouche, to bring world development into being, with justice and plenty for all.

shops, integral with a large industrial corporation; or is it better, at least in part, to have these firms as separate owner-operated firms, as vendors to large corporations?

The latter should be obvious. In an economy, when we go to things like infrastructure, which is a mandatory quality of improvement of the environment as a whole, then the state must be involved and the actual entrepreneurial quality of management by the state is not a premium, as long as we agree on the proper level of technology to be applied.

However, when we get into production, and particularly into the tool-making and tool-maintaining side of production—the area where the greatest amount of creative progress is made in technology—we require the greatest amount of concentration on private initiative and the smallest ratio of employment in administration, to employment in combined research and production functions—what I call research and development functions—as well as production.

So the farm is like that. To maintain progress in agriculture requires the same principle as in the middle-sized, high-tech industry, in which the entrepreneurial farmer, with the least amount of administrative cost in the farm structure, is the vehicle by which technology and technological improvements are mediated, to produce a quality product. And thus, we need the family farm or the equivalent—essentially the family farm—as the predominant institution of quality agriculture.

Obviously, there will tend to be a great deal of specialization in hydroponic/aeroponic agricultural pro-

duction, because of the capital investment which will tend to delimit. However, there will be also an intelligent application, a diversification, in order to utilize the capital more efficiently, and to hedge and balance against contingencies.

For example, we saw the idiocy of compelling farmers to choose between growing feed and feeding cattle, things like that. We need a diversified agriculture. The degree of diversification is not something which should be debated. The point is, the general idea: We want the advantage of the specialization, with diversification, and we want that potential for diversificaiton maintained actively within the unit farm. So the farmer should be diversified, at least to a small degree, in order to become *potentially* diversified, in a significant practice at some later date, as may be required.

The downsizing of farming in general is indicated by the very nature of farming.

We have seen the megafarm in the communist world, and the idea that so-called capitalist management in the West, can do a better job than the communists did, cannot be proved. There's not much of a case to be made for that.

The essential problem, as we see in former East Germany, we see in Czechoslovakia, we see in areas of the former Soviet Union, is that the transfer from the family farm to the megafarm, was the most significant factor of the agricultural disaster in those parts of the world.

Finally, just one additional comment on the subject of parity prices.

Farmers have been largely brainwashed on this subject of parity prices—that is, those who think they don't need it. They find every argument in the world to go against parity price.

The principle should be, that the parity price applies to the farmer, not the grain dealer or the grain speculator. It's at the farm gate, essentially. Plus, the discount of the parity price, is at the farm gate. And that price at the gate, within the total parity structure, that percentage of the total parity structure which represents farm product at the gate—that part is the part that must be paid to the farmer.

Now as to how this relates to mega-growth, or being competitive with mega-farming, that's a matter of tax policy. And we have, presently, an insane tax policy.

So, we should have sane regualtion, which is parity price regulation policy and a sane tax policy and a sane investment tax credit policy applied to agriculture as well as to industry.

How To Tell the Future

by Lyndon H. LaRouche, Jr.

Forget the faked market statistics. The past week's reports of the troubles afflicting leading Swiss banks, have crushed the previously lingering hopes among the professionals, that the onrushing, global financial crash which I have forecast might still be prevented.

Compulsive gamblers and all other desperately wishful fools aside, the past two weeks insiders' reports, have shown, that serious market analysts are worrying less about the market, than what happens to their personal physical security, when it might be the turn of some fellow in their office to uncork a wild shooting spree.

Consider some typical facts. First, the British monarchy, which presently dominates more than ninety percent of the world's present, international financial system, has announced internal military-security plans, its operation "Surety," anticipating a violent social crisis expected for the United Kingdom during the period from September 9, 1999, through the end of the year. Meanwhile, an international conference of psychiatrists, meeting in Hamburg, Germany, this past week, examined the deadly mental-health problems lurking, too often unsuspected, among people speculating in the world's financial markets.[1]

Around the world, the warning-signs are abundant. The Japan "yen carry trade," which was a key factor in the August-October 1998 near-meltdown of the world's financial system, is, once again, a bubble near the bursting-point. Now, the "gold carry trade," launched just this past Spring, has joined the "yen carry trade," among notable motives for panic in relevant financier circles. The "Euro," which had been collapsing in price since it was launched, at the beginning of 1999, is being propped up by the money fleeing into Europe from the U.S.A. That recent flight of investments out of the U.S., was encouraged by talk of a much feared, upcoming Wall Street financial collapse, which many financial analysts are saying, openly, may reach levels of between 25% and 40%, or more, below current prices.[2]

Given the present level of collapse in the general moral quality of the U.S. and European populations, in particular, over the course of the recent decades, there is a great likelihood, that under the kinds of sudden financial crises and their effects which we must expect now, there will be sudden eruptions of both spontaneous and orchestrated forms of extreme, homicidal violence, by individuals and mobs of various sorts. Wiser minds say, "Forget the financial system; it's almost as good as gone. Worry about what happens when the financial system goes under, and that very soon."

Meanwhile, all of the key physical measures of foreign trade balances, production, and per-capita market-basket physical income of the U.S. economy, and those of the rest of the Americas, Africa, and Europe, are down—way down by comparison with 1987-1989, and also with the 1970s. The looting of the physical assets of basic economic infrastructure, farms, factories, and net savings of households, in a desperate effort of financial interests to keep the financial bubble from collapsing, has brought these looted sectors of the real economy, way, way down, and falling rapidly.

Forget the lying statistics fabricated and issued by certain Federal Reserve System, U.S. Government, and like sources. Behind the faked figures, the real data, on both financial markets and the real economy, are not only down, down, down, but represent the period since February 1999 as the deepest down-turn of the 1990s so far. Look at the increasing spread between discount-rates on corporate and U.S. Treasury bonds, for exam-

1. The World Conference of Psychiatrists, meeting in Hamburg, Germany in mid-August, discussed the "Irrationality of the Stock Market Mania" as part of its official proceedings. See also, Lyndon H. LaRouche, Jr., "Star Wars and Littleton," **EIR**, July 2, 1999.

2. Other, circumstantially confirmed operations have used such sources of encouragement to attempt to fix the value of the Euro, somewhat upward, at a desired short-term level.

ple, to understand why leading financial institutions' reading of the real figures—not the faked statistics admired by the **Wall Street Journal**—has the top circles trembling in fear.

Do not be duped by the recent, cultish "millennium bug" side-show, the so-called "Y2K" panic. I always regarded Cobol as a costly folly, even back during the early 1960s, but that is not the cause of any danger to the world financial system come January 1, 2000. The reason a mountain—a virtual Mount Everest—of cheap credit is being built up for the last four months of 1999, is not "Y2K." The carefully cultivated rumor, that this credit build-up is for "Y2K" problems, is simply a cover-up of the fact, that this build-up of a tidal wave of cheap, "printing press" money for the coming months, is actually in anticipation of a coming, global financial blow-out which is already a rotten-ripe potential of the existing world financial system. The only situation which might possibly occur, which would require financial bail-outs on the scale of the emergency funding now announced, would be the biggest financial crash in history, occurring before the end of this year.

The collapse in the real economy of nations—their physical economy, is to be seen as my "Triple Curve" depicts the characteristic feature of the post-1971 world economy [**Figure 1**]. In net effect, the real economy, the physical economy, of most of the world's area, has been looted at increasing rates, looted to feed a cancer-like financial sector.

That looting, is the means on which the continued existence of the present financial system depends. That diseased financial system, is a cancer feeding on the real economy, consuming that body, in its desperate effort to support the world's post-1971 "floating exchange-rate monetary system." During the past two decades, as the world's real economy has been looted, more and more, to feed that financial cancer, the world's financial system has been characterized by a financial fever of combined austerity measures, junk bond plun-

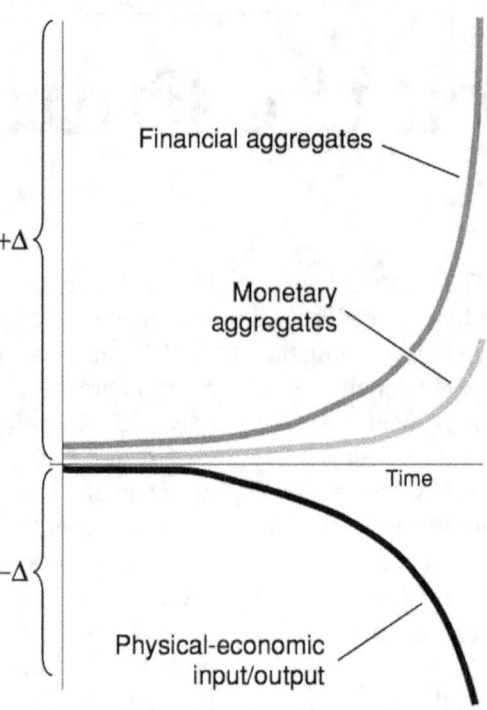

Figure 1
A Typical Collapse Function

Financial aggregates

+Δ

Monetary aggregates

Time

−Δ

Physical-economic input/output

derings, endless, "Woodstock-style" orgies of hedge-fund gambling, and sundry forms of predatory mergers and acquisitions.

Thus, in the U.S.A., the recent soaring of the Wall Street Dow-Jones Index and growth of mutual funds, for example, is not to be seen as a sign of prosperity, but directly the opposite. This so-called "boom"—in financial-asset-price hyperinflation—is actually the highly elevated fever that signals, and will bring about the financial system's approaching collapse and death, a sickness which has been named by Federal Reserve Chairman Alan Greenspan as "irrational exuberance," which Germany's former Chancellor Helmut Schmidt has recently described, more simply and appropriately, as psychotic behavior of the marketeers.[3]

Now, this past week, the announcement of major losses by leading Swiss banks, answers the question, "Where can I put my money for safety." Now, the answer seems to be, "Nowhere."[4] The big and smart money has already been engaged for some time, in a panicked effort to transform itself into gold and other physical assets of types expected to outlive the coming

3. In an interview with **Welt am Sonntag** published on Aug. 1, Helmut Schmidt said, "Presently, many people are enthusiastic about the United States. But these people do not realize that the stock market boom is totally over-valued, and that there are psychopaths who are driving the stocks upward. It is only a question of time for the boom to come to an end, and for stock values to go down the hill—just as it happened in Japan."

4. Rumors are flying of huge derivatives losses by the Union Bank of Switzerland and Crédit Suisse, wrote Zürich-based financial expert Heinz Brestel in an editorial in the German daily **Frankfurter Allgemeine Zeitung** on Aug. 12. According to these rumors, which resulted in sharp declines of UBS and CS stock prices on Aug. 10, the two biggest Swiss banks suffered from the dramatic increase of bond yields in recent months, and lost several billion dollars due to speculative transactions at the Cayman Islands.

Although the report was denied by representatives for the UBS, Crédit Suisse-First Boston, in deep trouble with its Japan operations, declined to affirm or deny. **EIR** sources affirmed the rumored "hit" suffered by Switzerland's banks to be true.

financial meltdown.

The urgent questions now, are only three. 1) How shall we keep the world's economic system—its real economy, its physical economy—functioning, under the condition that the financial systems of western Europe and the Americas are hopelessly bankrupt? 2) What radical changes must now be made, and that very quickly, to create a new monetary and financial system, and launch a genuine economic recovery? 3) From whom shall such urgently needed, expert advice come? Who has a proven record of competence on such economic issues?

In answer to all three of these questions, the following must be said.

Although there have been, and are other intelligent economists, the only statistically proven, scientific method of long-range economic forecasting is my own LaRouche-Riemann Method. The importance of this fact is shown by the evidence, that, even today, when the present world financial system is about to go over the cliff, there are still those, even among professional economists, who have come now to recognize, that the world's financial system is at the brink of new threats of "meltdown," but who, nonetheless, refuse, even now, to accept the most critical evidence as to the root-nature and causes of the presently ongoing, hyperinflationary mode of the monetary-financial collapse.

Like the Miniver Cheevy of Confederacy buff Teddy Roosevelt's favorite poem, these erring economists have their "reasons," as we shall point out here.

The issue today, goes way beyond, "Which economists made the best predictions—and, also, which, like Vice-President Al Gore, the worst?"[5]

Even when, during the months just ahead, the now inevitable collapse is being entered into the future history books, there will still be those, including many of today's leading names in the teaching of economics, who still raise their same old objection to my forecasts, this time to my proposed recovery program. They will base that continuing objection on the same old shopworn delusions, which have been the source of the time-worn incompetence of their past objections to my repeatedly confirmed forecast of the ongoing crash-trend. Up to this point, but for relatively rare exceptions, virtually all academic economists and govern-

ments have thus shown themselves to have been consistently wrong, not only in their forecasts, but, more importantly, in their incompetent definition of the way in which a modern economy functions.

Now, when the onrushing doom of the present world's financial system has become undeniable by all but those persons driven mad by this reality, the continuing issue will take a new form. Now, sane people will ask, "What is the correct *method* for forecasting, *either* a general financial crash, or an economic recovery from that crash?" I answer that question as follows.

1. What Can We Forecast?

Re-phrase the previous question: To what degree can economists—any economists—foretell the future? Can we expect that anyone could make a simple, unqualified, rational form of prediction, that a certain price will reach a certain exact level on a certain date?

The answer to that question is, "Mere accidents aside, obviously not." To at least a certain degree, human intervention can, within certain limits, willfully nullify any such unqualified prediction. Powerful governments can intervene to such effect. Those powerful financial agencies, which rig what is called, most curiously, the present-day "free market," rig prices of markets—and also governments—as their customary way of—for example—making a profit on price-speculation in so-called "futures markets."

Nonetheless, there have repeatedly been cases in which some people have accurately forecast financial collapses, as I have forecast the presently ongoing one. After each such forecasted crash, in my own and other confirmed forecasts, it has been shown, not only that the crash occurred as some economists had repeatedly forecast, but, also, that the crash was either caused, or, more often, merely triggered, by more or less exactly the factors on which the forecaster had based his earlier, qualified warnings.[6]

Nonetheless, despite such evidence of the precedents for the presently onrushing financial crash, such

---

5. On the record, Al Gore ranks with the absolutely worst, most illiterate personalities in matters of economic forecasting. Poor Al can not even predict past events competently.

6. The case of J.M. Keynes warning against the outcome of the policies adopted by the predatory victors at the Versailles conference, in his **The Economic Consequences of the Peace** (New York: Harcourt, Brace and Howe, 1920), is a useful example. Today, even economists with whom I disagree fundamentally, as I do with Keynes, may happen to draw sound conclusions about some of the medium- to long-term consequences of a bad policy.

as the examples of the Seventeenth-Century tulip bubble, or the early Eighteenth-Century John Law-style bubbles, there are some wild-eyed liberals and other mystics, who insist, still today, that if the market is kept as free as the Mont Pelerin Society's dogma of "the invisible hand" demands, everything will ultimately work out for the best, in exactly such unknowably wonderful ways, as those which snake-oil peddler Adam Smith insisted, exist only in some magical domain, beyond human comprehension.[7]

Yet, despite those wild-eyed believers in the greedy little god of "the invisible hand," each of my long-range forecasts, since the beginning of the 1960s, has been right exactly to the degree of precision which I have claimed for it. Then, if I am right in my method of long-term forecasting, as I have been so far, and if all economists who opposed me have been wrong, as they have been so far, can we assume, from that evidence alone, that my policies can forecast an economic recovery, and that the policies of my political opponents can not?

You answer that question: "Not necessarily so," and you are right to say so. Too many people are taken in by their own irrational faith in so-called experts. Credulous people look at experts as a child looks at a milk-cow. The cow produces milk by means which the child regards as more or less magical.[8] The cow is, for that child, an "expert" at producing milk. Most adults, like those children, look at the economics profession in a similarly irrational, more or less superstitious way, as secreting "expert" advice in the manner a cow produces milk. Superstitious people depend upon their faith in such experts, whether those supposed experts are competent or not.

You are right to insist, that other evidence, other than the simple fact that I have been proven expert in correctly forecasting such past developments, would be required to make my case. I summarize that other evidence here.

Successful forecasting is not so simple that it would allow us to make a bare, unqualified prediction. None-theless, there is a direct connection between the way I have successfully forecast the most important such crises of the past nearly thirty-five years,[9] and the way in which I am prepared to forecast the general direction of the happy results of the global monetary reform which I have named "a New Bretton Woods" system. When those facts are considered, my past successes do point toward the evidence which supports my argument for the way an economic recovery may be organized, even now.

The first fact to consider, is that *I have never simply "predicted" an event. I am no witch. I have always specified the qualified conditions under which a certain type of event was almost certain to occur, or not occur.* The source of the attempts to deprecate my forecasts, has usually been the obviously fraudulent way in which my would-be detractors have attempted to misrepresent my forecasts. I have always insisted, "Unless we change the presently prevailing policies in the following way, we are now approaching the following event as early as…" The self-styled "critic" usually became extremely agitated at that point, insisting that I predict a certain event as of a certain date, *whether the presently prevailing policy-trends, on which my forecast was based, were changed, or not.* In other words, the fraudulent argument of that would-be detractor, was his insistence that I practice magic, not scientific forecasting. That fraud has been typical of them.

All those defenders of so-called "liberal economics" insisted, that programs of deregulation, "free trade," and "globalization," would ensure a successful economy. They even insisted that a growth of the financial cancer, such as a rise in the Dow-Jones index, is a sign of healthy prosperity. The onrushing financial debacle has proven them all so terribly wrong on those points.

The second, related fraud from such quarters, has been the sophistry, "If you are right, then why do almost no economists agree with you?" My answer to that paralogism, is simple: "If the doctrines of all the most influential economists, to whom you refer, were not, not only incompetent, but indeed radically in error, the world's economy, which has been shaped by their advice, would not be in the desperate mess it is in today."

For example, remember, that I forecast, repeatedly,

---

7. Actually, as Al Gore's Wall Street financial backers could reveal to you, the only "invisible hand" in the U.S. economy, is Wall Street's hand, in your pocket. Adam Smith's (and Al Gore's) kookish definition of the "invisible hand," is to be found in his 1759 **The Theory of the Moral Sentiments**. From no later than 1763, Adam Smith was a lackey of Lord Shelburne, a member of the same stable of East India Company lackeys as Shelburne's Jeremy Bentham.

8. Of course, that child is a marvel of sanity when compared with the housewife, or others, who insist that it is the "free market," rather than the farm, which produces milk.

---

9. Since the British monetary devaluation of November 1967 and the dollar devaluation of March 1968.

beginning the end of the 1950s, that, *if the world's policy-shaping trends of the 1950s were continued into the middle of the 1960s*, the last half of the 1960s would experience a series of monetary crises, leading into a crash of the then-existing world monetary system. *Those global trends, which I had pinpointed by my studies of the economic policy-shaping of the 1953-1961 Eisenhower years, were continued as long-term trends, throughout most of the 1960s*, with the resulting November 1967 collapse of the British pound, and the March 1968 collapse of the U.S. dollar. Those crises, and the Penn-Central, Chrysler panic of 1970, were followed by the breakdown of the entire post-war, Bretton Woods monetary system in mid-August 1971.

That is typical of what I mean by the term "long-term forecasting."[10]

Note, that the reason my 1960-1971 forecast succeeded as it did, was that, even with the brief improvements in U.S. policy under President John F. Kennedy, the long-term trends of the 1960s were, overall, those I had adduced from the policy-trends of the 1954-1961 interval.

Recall, if you are young enough to have remembered, that, until mid-August 1971, virtually every academic economist teaching in U.S. universities had absolutely insisted that the so-called "built-in stabilizers" of the system made such a crash impossible. The irony of their folly was, that the so-called "built-in stabilizers" of the post-World War II IMF system had been the tough regulatory measures instituted under Franklin Roosevelt's "New Deal" and the pre-1958 phase of the post-war international monetary order. It was precisely those most essential "built-in stabilizers," which these economists were insisting be gutted.

Of course, then as now, there were also those witless gossips, who taught that financial crashes occur only because some people "talk us into one." So much for the kookish variety of Economics 101 taught to virtually every university student of the recent forty and more years!

Remember, if you are old enough to do so, that within the weeks immediately following the August 1971 break-up of the old Bretton Woods system, I issued a new long-term forecast, issued under the title

of "Depression Ahead?" I warned that, *if the new trends set up by President Nixon's foolish decision, the set up of the combination of austerity measures and a "floating exchange-rate monetary system," were the continued standards for policy-shaping*, the world economy, in its present, new, post-1971 form, would pass through a series of crises leading toward disintegration of the system as a whole. I indicated the causes underlying such a long-range forecast, by pointing to the role of the physical economy—the real economy—often more hidden than revealed by the published statistical portrait of the money economy.

That view of the policy-conflict between real economy—physical economy—and post-1971 monetary and financial policy, is now demonstrated fully to have been a correct assessment of what has happened over the subsequent nearly thirty years. That is the proverbial "bottom line" for what is happening now.

The lesson to be learned from those and my other successes in long-range forecasting, is, that *the ability to forecast long-range economic trends, depends upon a correct identification of the set of definitions, axioms, and postulates, which underlie the way in which successive, even radical changes in policy-making will be shaped over the relevant period ahead.* The only cause for the cyclical forms of financial crashes, is that influential people swindle governments, other economic institutions, and the population more widely, into blind faith in a certain "generally accepted" set of definitions, axioms, and postulates, a set of axiomatics which is, in fact, not only false, but, ultimately, more or less fatally so.

For example: The interrelated dogmas of "free trade" and "the invisible hand" are outrightly superstitious, anti-scientific dogmas, based on nothing but a combination of cheap parlor tricks and blind faith. The reason most people refuse to recognize that present trends in policy-making are leading toward a foreseeable crisis over the long-term, is that they refuse to recognize that their own beliefs are wishful self-delusions, rooted in false opinions about what they believe, and wish policy ought to be.

The only remedy for such an economic catastrophe, such as the presently ongoing doom of the world's present financial system, is to dump the existing set of "generally accepted" axiomatic assumptions, and adopt an appropriate new one. It is the refusal of institutionalized opinion to recognize a wrong prevailing policy, a wrong generally accepted opinion, which causes a society to

---

10. Generally, in my usages, a short-term forecast is for a lapse of time of up to two years, usually one year or less. A medium-term forecast covers a period of not less than three to five years. A long-term forecast usually signifies a lapse of time of not less than seven years, and may include a period of up to thirty or more years.

continue travelling down the road to some awful new crisis, and it is through the tragic insistence of that opinion, that we must continue that misguided belief, that generally accepted opinion destroys entire nations, or nearly so.

Here, I shall show you how that works. Once you have understood the proof of the point I have just made, you will know the gist of the way in which successful economic forecasting works.

I shall address this proposition on two levels. First, I shall describe the problem of defining the physical principles involved in constructing a forecast. Second, I shall explain why it is not sufficient to consider only those physical principles. One must also focus upon the political-cultural factors which will cause societies to continue to cling to opinions which will, alternately, save them, or ruin them, the latter option almost up to the very end, or beyond.

A Lesson from Geometry

Ancient and modern witch-doctors' reading of animal entrails, Professor Milton Friedman, and ouija boards put aside, modern civilization inherited the idea of a rational kind of economic forecasting from physical science.

The scientific forecasting of any kind of future physical events, began in prehistoric times, with the construction of solar-astronomical calendars, and with the use of related methods for transoceanic and related navigation. As you might observe simply by reading an ancient design of the Zodiac, what such ancient astronomers and navigators observed, was the regularity of changes in positions which could be measured, not as straight-line connections, but as angular movements.

Those ideas of forecasting, which we have from such earlier historic societies as the Vedic calendars of Central Asia, the astronomy of Egypt, and the ancient, pre-Roman, Greek and Hellenistic astronomers and navigators, are the point of origin for the notion of *universal physical laws* which extended European civilization has inherited, and developed still further, up to the present day.

Never let sophists' tricks mislead you into overlooking the obvious. What does angular measurement in astronomy and navigation mean? It means that even the earliest stages of physical science began with the notion, that the laws of the universe describe the lawful distance between two observed points *in physical space-time*, as an *intrinsically* curved pathway, not that

straight-line pathway proposed by such fellows as Paolo Sarpi's personal household lackey Galileo Galilei, or by Abbot Antonio Conti's "Trilby" Isaac Newton.[11] In other words, a curved orbital pathway of a planet, moon, or comet, is not the result of forces acting along straight lines, at a distance. Regular orbital pathways are the result of the fact, first proved empirically by Kepler, and later by Carl Gauss, that physical space-time itself is intrinsically curved, and that each orbit is defined by its own specific, inherently curved, orbital characteristic of the Kepler-Leibniz-Gauss-Riemann type.[12]

The ancient Greeks, such as Plato, defined the physical universe in terms of spherical action, rather than straight-line pathways.[13] Cardinal Nicholas of Cusa founded modern experimental physical science on an elementary fresh proof of that point, using geometry.[14] After Nicholas of Cusa, Kepler was the next modern thinker who revived the ancient, pre-Roman, Greek civilization's knowledge, that the Earth orbited the Sun.[15] On such premises, Kepler founded the first modern mathematical physics on the evidence which confirmed Plato's **Timaeus**. After Kepler's proofs for the Solar System, Huyghens, Leibniz, Bernouilli, Gauss, Riemann, et al., defined regular lawful action in our universe on the basis of regular action of non-con-

11. The correspondence of Galileo refers explicitly to the fact that Galileo's ideas about science were those given to him, by personal instruction of the powerful Venetian Paolo Sarpi, who employed Galileo as a lackey of his personal household. It was the same Sarpi who used England's Sir Francis Bacon as one of his agents, and the same Galileo who educated Bacon's intimate Thomas Hobbes in mathematics. Newton was elevated from relative obscurity by the intervention of the Paris-based, powerful agent of Venice, Abbot Antonio Conti. It was Conti, acting through a Europe-wide network of his controlled assets, such as Dr. Samuel Clarke and Voltaire, who created the Eighteenth-Century myth of Isaac Newton.

12. This is the Kepler-Gauss-Riemann notion which Albert Einstein adopted as a point of reference for his own later, more refined notions of General Relativity in a Riemannian form of physical space-time which is "self-bounded."

13. See Plato's treatment of the Platonic Solids, in his **Timaeus**, in **Plato: Vol. IX,** Loeb Classical Library (Cambridge, Mass.: Harvard University Press, 1975).

14. **De docta ignorantia (On Learned Ignorance)**, trans. by Jasper Hopkins as **Nicholas of Cusa on Learned Ignorance** (Minneapolis: Arthur M. Banning Press, 1985). Cusa's exposure of a crucial error in Archimedes' method for defining the ratio of the perimeter of a circle to the circle's diameter, thus defined regular action in the universe in terms of regular curvature, rather than straight-line connections.

15. Johannes Kepler emphasized his crucial indebtedness to the scientific discoveries of Nicholas of Cusa, and to the students of Cusa's founding of modern science, Luca Pacioli and Leonardo da Vinci.

stant curvature—and not as straight-line action, not as Galileo and Newton defined "action at a distance."

Thus, when these and related, most crucial facts of the history of physical science are taken into account, we must agree that the usual way most European classrooms today teach Classical Euclidean geometry is fraudulent in effect, even when such bad instruction is negligent, rather than intentionally a hoax. Most recent decades' classrooms have taught Euclid in ways which were directly contrary to the basis on which the ancient Greeks developed Euclidean geometry, the latter which was the same basis used by Plato and such successors of Plato as Eratosthenes. Today's commonplace falsification of Euclid was done in the effort to make it appear that Euclidean geometry agreed with what are called the "radically reductionist" doctrines of such fellows as Aristotle, Galileo, Descartes, and Newton, rather than the most crucial empirical evidence of both known ancient and modern physical science.

In the passing century's U.S. secondary and university classrooms, for example, Euclid was usually mistaught in ways intended to suggest, as most generally accepted classroom mathematics does, that one must accept as given, a set of definitions of space and time implied by the fraudulent assumption defended by caught-out hoaxster Maupertuis and his defender, Euler, that the shortest distance in physical space-time is along what most classroom teaching of Euclidean geometry defines for the simple-minded as a straight line. That same, false, but generally accepted classroom mathematics, is the basis upon which all incompetent forms of statistical economic forecasting have been based, up to the present time.

Competent modern physical science rejects absolutely the widely taught misrepresentation of the Leibniz calculus, the linear fallacy presented to credulous students as the "limit theorem" of the celebrated hoaxster Augustin Cauchy. This is the same fraud introduced by such earlier hoaxsters as Galileo Galilei, René Descartes, Isaac Newton, Leonhard Euler, et al. The same hoax was defended even by a modern physicist as famous as Professor Felix Klein, in Klein's exaggerated claims for the work of Euler, Hermite, and Lindemann respecting the definition of the so-called transcendental. All of these fallacious systems are based upon the assumption that all physical relations in the universe can be ultimately derived, mathematically, from the absurd assumption that the straight line is the pathway of least action in physical space-time.

A Hellenistic Greek astronomer in Alexandria, Egypt, in the Second Century B.C. "The principled notion," writes LaRouche, "that man's increase of power in the universe is orderable, is defined in respect to the 'clock' provided by regular curvature in astronomical processes."
www.arttoday.com

Not only are linear systems false, in and of themselves. Such beliefs as Cauchy's widely taught, radically linearized version of the taught calculus, also act as very efficient delusions. In their character as not merely misled persons' wrong beliefs, but vicious, systemic delusions, they not only uphold false beliefs, but blind the victims of such delusions, such as the followers of Bertand Russell and his clones Norbert Wiener and John von Neumann, to the most elementary principles of scientific progress, including those of competent mathematical forms of long-range economic forecasting.

It is in precisely this area of scientific method, that the supposed secrets of successful long-range economic forecasting lie. This is even more true for forecasting of successful designs for economic recoveries and growth, than it is indispensable for understanding the causes of crises such as the presently unfolding one.

By "scientific work," including the work of long-range economic forecasting, one signifies a body of knowledge premised upon a process of discovery of ever more, experimentally validatable, universal physical principles. This signifies not only the process of discovery of such validatable principles, but a view of that willful relationship of mankind to the universe as a whole, which is based upon the methods by means of which such discoveries of universal principle have been generated, up to any present time.

In effect, a linear mathematical view of physical science suppresses the most crucial features of the work of physical science, the work of discovering and validating universal physical principles. Once one understands this issue, and only then, is it possible to understand the deep reasons for my relatively unique success as a long-term forecaster.

Faiths Contrary To Reason

As Bernhard Riemann emphasizes the crucial point, in the opening of his celebrated 1854 habilitation dissertation, in Europe until that time, the teaching and practice of geometry were based on purely arbitrary, axiomatic assumptions concerning the meaning of the terms space, time, and matter. These false assumptions were defined as *a priori*, or "self-evident" definitions and axioms, arbitrary assumptions, such as those of Immanuel Kant's series of *Critiques*, customarily superimposed upon reality, rather than derived from it.

For our purposes here, these false assumptions, such as those of both Kant and G.W.F. Hegel, are fairly classified under the heading of "faiths contrary to reason." What I shall describe in the following paragraphs may shock you, but understanding those several points will enable you to understand why relatively few practicing economists have been effective long-range forecasters.

The fatally flawed, relatively popular method, which is derived from blind faith in such axiomatic assumptions, locates observed phenomena within a purely fictitious domain of space, time, and matter, as that conjectured domain is defined by the purely arbitrary, straight-line definitions and axioms of a generally accepted classroom version of geometry in particular, and of mathematics more broadly. To the degree that the relatively more popular classroom methods of mathematical argument (e.g., formulas), are subsumed under a principle of universal deduction, such a math-

ematics, based upon the array of definitions and axioms of a quasi-Euclidean geometry, confuses the victim's mind to the following effect.

The victim assumes falsely, that the arbitrarily assumed, deductive connection among those sense-certainties treated, respectively, as cause and effect, represents the primary form of physical relations in space-time, as that of straight-line connections. That victim tends to assume that the relationship between the two phenomena is either percussive, or of the form of "action at a distance." Hence, all such more popular ways of thinking, including many falsely called "non-linear" today, are axiomatically linear, "ivory tower" systems.

That kind of commonly taught, more popular assumption, is the first cause for the pervasive falseness inhering in today's teaching of generally accepted classroom mathematics, and of statistical economic forecasting. This cause is rooted in the adoption of an arbitrary set of *a priori* definitions and axioms.[16] These definitions and axioms have a systemic, pernicious effect on the thinking of the victim, even if that student is unaware of the planting and existence of such induced axiomatic assumptions in his, or her own deeper, axiomatically controlling mental processes.

The second, complementary source of falseness, is the popular failure to accept the authority of experimentally validated universal physical principles, as the axioms which must replace, entirely, the *a priori* sets of definitions and axioms which are more commonly taught in universities, still today. This popular ideological contamination of mental life, is the problem which must be understood, and conquered, as a precondition for any rational comprehension of the means by which a generalized increase in the average productive powers of labor is made possible. The proof of the importance of overcoming this commonplace, and extremely important problem, is expressed in either the case in which increase of those productive powers is suppressed, or, conversely, happily, in which the increase of such powers is effectively fostered.

First, review summarily the connections of modern economic progress to scientific and technological prog-

---

16. The doctrines of "mathematical economics" derived from a melding of the legacy of Leon Walras and the positivist Lausanne School, with the systems of solutions for simultaneous linear inequalities which charlatans have derived from John von Neumann's and Oskar Morgenstern's **The Theory of Games and Economic Behavior**, are examples of this kind of folly.

ress. After that, we shall examine the more complex case, of the way in which the matters of both scientific and social progress are interconnected in determining the success or failure of a modern economy.

Thus, first, we focus upon the connection of productive powers of labor to scientific and technological progress as such. Mastering some of these points will take a bit of work, but, considering the terrible consequences of continuing not to understand this point, the chore is manageable, with a little study, and very much worthwhile.

Although the crucial features of the development of modern mathematical-physical science, can be traced to Kepler, Leibniz, and their contemporary co-thinkers, the crucial challenge was not mastered, until the successive work of Carl Gauss and Bernhard Riemann in defining the hypergeometric principles of a physical geometry expressed in the form known as a *multiply-connected manifold*. Don't let the strange words frighten you. Two distinguishing characteristics of all such Gauss-Riemann manifolds, are of the relatively greatest interest for the subject of long-term forecasting.[17]

First, that Riemann threw out all those misleading definitions, axioms, and postulates of an aprioristic formal geometry, and replaced these by an open-ended array of experimentally validated universal physical principles. Nothing but such experimentally validated, universal physical principles, was allowed. This restriction included the notions of space, time, and matter themselves; no purely mathematical definitions of these terms were permitted.

Second, Riemann, following Gauss's work on the general notion of curved surfaces, insisted that the multiple-connectedness of any such specific geometry is expressed by a unique characteristic of action, replacing the so-called "Pythagorean" measure used to compare a so-called simple Euclidean formal geometry with a spherical geometry [**Figure 2**]. The same function of a characteristic of any manifold applies, as Gauss and Riemann each show, to defining the higher orders of curvature by means of which one manifold is

Figure 2
Euclidean vs. Spherical Geometry

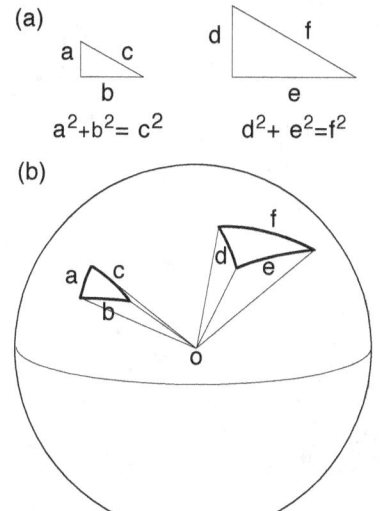

(a)

$a^2 + b^2 = c^2$ $d^2 + e^2 = f^2$

(b)

The Pythagorean Theorem

On a plane, the shortest distance between two points is a line, which can be measured by the Pythagorean Theorem (a). But on a sphere, the shortest distance between two points is an arc of a great circle, and has to be measured as a combination of angular displacements. The Pythagorean Theorem does not hold on a sphere, because the sum of the angles of a triangle is variable, depending upon the size of the triangle (b).

distinguished experimentally from another.

The latter characteristic of actual economies, can not be adduced by formal mathematical analysis of the manifold itself. It must be adduced by the methods of experimental physics. It can not be "proven" at the blackboard, or by a computer system; it must be measured in the laboratory, or in the actual performance of a real-life physical economy.[18]

That means the following.

Whether within the domain of the physical space-time laboratory, or astronomy, as such, or in the relative change in economic physical-space-time caused by introducing a newly discovered universal physical principle to technology, the addition of a new universal physical principle to either the scientific investigation, or to human technological practice, results in a change in the physical-geometry of man's efficient relationship to the universe around us. The Gauss-Riemann manifold shows us how to understand the practical implications of adding such validated new physical principles of this axiomatic quality.

In the field of astrophysics, for example, the inclusion of a newly validated such principle, such as Kepler's discovery of the elliptical characteristic of the

17. Riemann's accomplishment is so deeply indebted to the preceding work of his mentor Gauss, that what we term a Riemannian manifold must be better named a Gauss-Riemann manifold. In that way, Riemann's unique contribution to the science of physical geometry is securely and precisely located, both historically and functionally.

18. i.e., the distinction on which Nicholas of Cusa premised the founding of modern experimental physics. The kind of experimental design required, a so-called *unique experiment*, need merely be mentioned for our purposes in the present report.

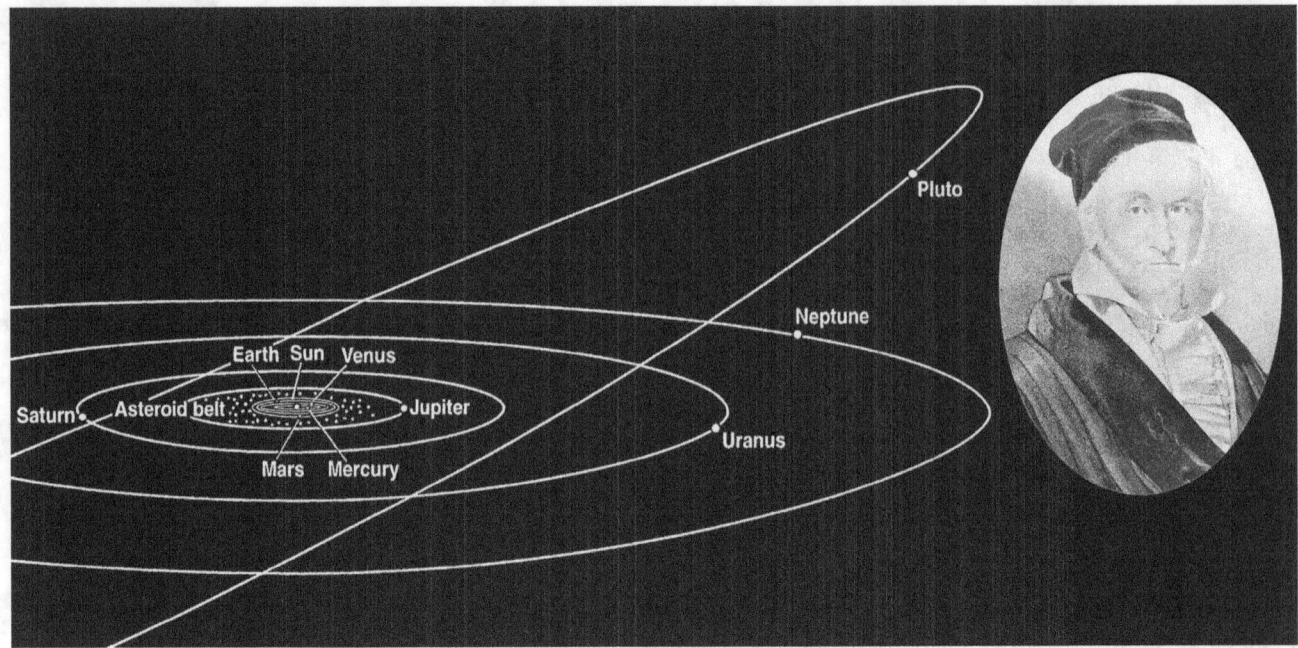

"Gauss's corroboration of the orbit of the asteroid Ceres as the orbit of a missing, formerly exploded planet specified by Kepler, is a demonstration of the exhaustive approach to that measurement of a characteristic, non-constant curvature of a regular process, which is demanded by Riemann's dissertation."

planetary orbits, requires us to measure the characteristic features of the whole domain in a new way.

Kepler reacted to this discovery in two leading ways. First, he redefined characteristic interconnections within the Solar System according to the implications of this discovery. Second, he measured the characteristic interval of action to be associated with those implications, just as Riemann specifies this necessity in the conclusion of his habilitation dissertation. Gauss's corroboration of the orbit of the asteroid Ceres as the orbit of a missing, formerly exploded planet specified by Kepler, is a demonstration of the exhaustive approach to that measurement of a characteristic, non-constant curvature of a regular process, which is demanded by Riemann's dissertation.[19]

In the field of physical economy, we have a case which is more complex. Limiting ourselves, for the moment, to the physical side of the matter as such, we have the following.

Provided that we revise the physical processes of an economy, including both its modes of production and basic economic infrastructure, in ways conforming to the discovery of a new family of physical principles—a new manifold—the characteristic result of a constant quantity of individual human effort will be changed for that national economy as a whole. In the case of technological progress, the change will be a gain in the ratio of total physical output to the actually incurred costs of production.[20] Those comparisons are to be made in terms of market-baskets, rather than such inherently unscientific standards of measure as mere money-prices.

This gain in rate of growth, per capita and per square kilometer, for that economy as a whole, is a measure of a change, to a higher physical state, in the characteristic curvature of that economy's economic physical-space-time curvature.

Thus, if we can ensure that such validated discoveries of principle occur, and that the economy is modified in the way these discoveries imply, there will be a re-

19. Cf. Jonathan Tennenbaum and Bruce Director, "How Gauss Determined the Orbit of Ceres," **Fidelio**, Summer 1998. Kepler's discovery of the principle of gravitation was derived as a by-product of his derivation of what are usually misnamed Kepler's Three Laws. The combination of these three principles shows that we must measure the characteristic action of a Solar System in which elliptical planetary orbits exist, in a different way than were the orbits simply circular. The resulting difference in characteristic is expressed in terms of a measurable magnitude known as gravitation.

20. Whether those long-term trends in rising "equilibrium costs" are met in the short term, or not.

sulting, generally increased rate of physical-economic growth, per capita and per square kilometer.

Similarly, if we suppress the continuation of such realized scientific and technological progress, or even go to such extremes as reversing previously introduced gains in technology—as the U.S.A. has done repeatedly during the recent twenty-eight years—a catastrophic trend toward collapse of the economy must result. Such a catastrophe must occur, either if a deliberate anti-science policy was imposed, as has been done to U.S. policy-shaping, increasingly, since 1966-1972 changes in long-term economic policy, or if such a disinvestment in the prerequisites of scientific and technological progress was imposed through the impact of financial and monetary policies, as has been done since 1971, especially since 1977.

Once those two mutually reenforcing sets of policy-changes were introduced, it became virtually impossible to generate a national real-economy profit in the way which had been characteristic of the American System of political-economy in all successful periods since U.S. Treasury Secretary Alexander Hamilton.

As the earlier investments in scientific and technological progress wore out, and as the quality of productivity-related and other education in schools and universities worsened since the mid-1970s, the only remaining source of profit for the U.S. economy as a whole, became, in effect, "carpet-bagging," looting of preexisting wealth. This took the form either of stealing from other nations and peoples, as the British Empire had done that traditionally, or looting our own population and existing, previous investments in basic economic infrastructure, development of the labor-force's households, and production as such.

The murder of more and more of the U.S. population through such measures as the Gingrich-Gore "welfare reform" of 1996, and the recent, deliberately murderous "reforms" in "cost-efficient managed health-care," are to be viewed, together with "outsourcing," as typical. They typify those financial accountant's methods, by means of which our national productivity per capita and per square kilometer, and our population itself, have been looted and ruined, even murdered, for the greater glory and profit of an increasingly damned few, Wall Street and kindred, profiteering parasites.

Whether these ruinous measures were taken in the name of "the environment," "promoting free trade," "deregulation," or "globalization," the overall effect was the same.

2. Self-destruction as a Social Process

The cultural change which led to the present process of self-destruction by the United States, and also other nations, emerged as a mass phenomenon, the so-called "cultural paradigm-shift" of the late 1960s, during the 1964-1972 interval, more specifically. By the early 1980s, this process of national economic self-destruction, as I have just described it in the preceding section of this report, was established as the seemingly almost incontestable, prevailing trend in cultural change.

Thereafter, more and more people departed the ranks of those who had caused the dumping of President Carter, as an expression of their angered opposition to the evil policy-changes of the Trilateral Commission's Carter-Administration period.[21] More and more of these former Carter opponents, went over to applying, in effect, for employment as virtual paid agents of the very same destruction, such as that launched by Carter's appointment of Federal Reserve Chairman Paul Volcker, which had earlier ruined the U.S. economy, and, for many, their lives, too. The recent, wide participation of a very large part of the nation's family households in mutual-funds adventures, typifies the way in which more and more of our current population of credit-card slaves, has since turned against our nation, and, in the end, against themselves as well.

Thus, it is broadly the case with much of our population, that the same system which they had opposed, until the beginning of the 1980s, became the virtual "foreign occupying power" which they had decided to support, from about the middle of the 1980s onward. That is how a virtual majority of the actually voting citizens of the U.S. came to decide, either through despair, or other expressions of personal moral corruption—i.e., cultural pessimism, to participate in destroying their nation, and themselves. "Look, I can't worry about what happens to the world as a whole; I have to concentrate on the interests of myself, my family, and my local

---

21. Never forget that both Carter and George Bush were among those initially coopted into David Rockefeller's Trilateral Commission. It was during that period, preceding the Trilateral Commission's election of its hand-crafted Jimmy Carter as President, that the core of the policies of the future Carter and Bush administrations were crafted by a team headed by Cyrus Vance, Zbigniew Brzezinski, et al. This was a project of the British Foreign Office's creation, known as New York Council on Foreign Relation's "Project 1980s" reports of 1975-1976, subsequently published, under a Lilly Foundation grant, by McGraw-Hill.

neighborhood." That is the face of deep moral pessimism, deep moral corruption, the face of angry individuals occupied chiefly with destroying their nation, and themselves.

That is why so many today have so much to fear from those day-traders and the like, who might become the run-amok killers of tomorrow morning. Such times of sheer horror proliferate, when the moral fiber of a people has been ruined in the way so many Americans, and others, have been affected by the economic and

---

The recent, wide participation of a very large part of the nation's family households in mutual-funds adventures, typifies the way in which more and more of our current population of credit-card slaves, has since turned against our nation, and, in the end, against themselves as well.

---

social policy-shaping trends of the recent three decades.

If you did not see this very ugly side of the decadent role of many among your fellow-citizens, you neither understood what was being done to this nation, nor what so many among you, through your own folly, were contributing to doing to yourselves.

That accelerating moral decay among a very large ration of our post-1980 citizenry, was reflected in its similarity to the mentality of a defeated and conquered population, which has decided to seek a more secure personal life in a "Faustian pact" of service to the apparent occupying power, perhaps, in some cases, Satan himself.[22]

We have seen this recently, in the case of the so-called Russian liberals who have sought lavishly unearned livings in lackey-like service to those foreign carpet-baggers who have taken over the richest chunks of loot to be extracted from the quasi-defeated nation.

---

22. Since we are on the subject of the rooting of knowable political principles in the principles of Classical art, here, the case of Goethe's **Faust** is among the more revealing insights into a cultural phenomenon which has been the subject of special attention in Germany, but which is applicable to the population of most of all Europe, and also the U.S.A. today. The key to Goethe's use of Christopher Marlowe's subject, **Dr. Faustus**, for insight into the principled moral flaw of a real-life German Faust, typifies the case of the morally depraved person who believes, that he can cling to the pleasures and profits of his corrupt practices, and have a wonderful ending, too. Faust has not degenerated to the much lower moral level of a typical existentialist, but he is nonetheless the type of person one should be ashamed to be, ashamed enough to stop being that.

The typical self-styled "patriotic Americans" of today, such as Georgia's U.S. Representative Barr, are not far behind the notorious, mafia-linked, unpatriotic liberals of Russia, in the depraved things they do to their own nation and its posterity.

Recognizing this factor of moral decay taking over the U.S. population itself, had been key for my successful forecasting of the process which had unfolded, earlier, in the developments of the 1960-1971 interval. It was also key to my insight into the virtual political inevitability of the global financial crisis striking the world today. I focus on the narrower aspect of the latter developments, the moral decay within the U.S. population itself.

Are You Predictable?

You tell me, that you make up your own mind. How, in Heaven or on Earth, could I have been so rude, and also so efficiently insightful, as ever to doubt that you do?

In fact, most of the time, and on most of the really important decisions you make, you rarely, if ever, actually made up your own mind. That fact, however its mention embarrasses you, is what most of the mass media, crooked politicians, and pollsters and forecasters generally rely upon, in the way in which they win their incomes from the credulity of those suckers—the majority of the population—who, in recent times, have seldom actually make up their own minds about almost anything of relevance to the future of our nation and its economy.

Unless you help me wake up their sleeping minds, most people today actually know almost nothing, and will probably know even less as time passes. In place of knowing, they have adopted opinions, which, they believe, will cause other people to like them, or perhaps simply not dislike them, or even bring tangible forms of rewards, such as sex, money, and relatively higher rank in some real, or even merely imagined, social pecking-order. The popular cult of Hollywood "stars," is a leading example of this sort of widespread corruption of the population.[23] We see that in the substitution of "text-

---

23. Giuseppe Verdi, for example, was an Italian patriot in the tradition of Dante Alighieri, who used the model of tragedy as typified for him by Shakespeare and Schiller, to elevate the minds of Italians to the quality needed for citizenship of a true national republic. How many of the audiences for Verdi today, for example, cheer the play, rather than the individual "star performers"? How many in the audience respond to the powerful, important ideas which Verdi built into the design of his operas, for example? Yes, the leading performers must carry a heavy

book learning" in schools, and the related use of methods of induced behavioral modification, as borrowed from animal training, for shaping the expressed opinions of both children and adults.

This pathological state of affairs, is shown most clearly, if one attempts to provoke individuals into submitting to a Socratic form of "knowing experience." Typically, they resist such provocations, rebuking the would-be Socrates, "I already have my own opinion." The conversation usually breaks up at that point, the opinionated person parading off, triumphantly, knowing nothing.

That same sucker-principle, is what has made a farce of the very names of "democracy" and "democratic methods," inside the presently Gored-out, but hopefully reformable leadership of our U.S. Democratic National Committee, in our Federal courts, or around the world today. You, with rare exceptions, despite your insisting that you make up your own mind, represent, at least typically, the most suggestible, most predictable victims of manipulation of both mass and individual U.S. opinion (in particular) of the entire Twentieth Century!

That, obviously, must change, and that very quickly. Otherwise, this nation will not live to see the bright side of the coming, Twenty-First Century. Here, in this concluding portion of my present report, I limit our attention to the way in which both hidden, and not-so-hidden popular, axiomatic assumptions control the way in which the individual members of society are controlled, to the degree of making mass behavior, including the behavior of the economy, usually so pathetically, tragically predictable lately, over periods as long as decades, or even longer.

This prompts us to revisit, briefly, the subject of Euclidean geometry. In this report so far, we have identified the governing role of axiomatic assumptions about space, time, and matter, in shaping our policies of action, or inaction, toward the physical universe. Now, we must turn our attention to the analogous role of other kinds of axiomatic assumptions, about both man and society, which act to shape political and other opinions in much the same way that the definitions, axioms, and postulates of physical geometry do.

The two kinds of assumptions, those referencing physical geometry, and those referencing man and society as such, combine to form whatever governing "mind-set" usually controls the way in which individuals and entire nations shape their policies of practice. It is the trends generated by the impact of these "mind-sets," which make human mass behavior as ominously, tragically predictable as it has been, over periods of decades or longer. That appreciation of the role of "mind-sets" is key to all successful long-range forecasting.

As you may have learned, from my earlier published locations, it has been, so far, since nearly a half a century, my unique contribution to scientific thought, especially to the science of physical economy, to recognize that we must not separate the axiomatic assumptions of physical science from those axiomatic qualities of assumption which are best expressed by the greatest compositions of what are rigorously defined as Classical art-forms. In other words, I made the first successful break, through the barrier separating what England's C.P. Snow, for example, defined as "the two cultures."[24]

I summarize that connection, as I have repeatedly stated it in earlier published locations, and then show the specific application of that connection to the matter of economic forecasting of either catastrophe or economic renaissance.

The reader must think of the "axioms" of universal Classical artistic principles, as analogous in form of function to the validated universal physical principles of a Gauss-Riemann hypergeometry. For our purposes here, it is sufficient to consider but a few such axioms.

1. The Prime Axiom.

The first step toward the needed solution of the so-called "two cultures" dichotomy, is found, with a wonderfully ironic appropriateness, in the first chapter of **Genesis**. Man and woman are each made in the image of the Creator, designed by Him to rule within His universe. The solution to the "two cultures" dichotomy, lies in stating that in the form of an axiomatic principle as to the form of the function so described by **Genesis**. As Leibniz said, it is a very good beginning.

---

portion of the play, but it is the ensemble as a whole, including the musicians in the pit, who contribute to that total effect which the play (e.g., opera) as a whole must convey to the moral and intellectual uplifting of both the players and the audience.

24. C.P. Snow, **Two Cultures and, the Scientific Revolution** (London and New York: Cambridge University Press, 1993 reprint). Obviously, what I have done is no more than complete a needed stage in the way the greatest philosophers, typified by Plato and Leibniz, have attempted, over no less than thousands of years to date, to understand a common underlying basis in the interrelationship between man and nature. I was merely the first to make the connections to which they pointed, as explicit as a science of physical economy requires.

The nature of man, and of man's relationship to the universe, lies in a principle of change, the kind of principle which can not be stated in the terms of any merely deductive schema. The change in question, is *the process of mankind's increase of its physical power to command the universe, as measured in human-demographic terms, per capita, and per square kilometer of the Earth's surface-area.*

That power is located in a continuing, progressively ordered accumulation of discovery of validatable, universal physical principles, such as the notion of a regular ordering of astronomical changes in observed position. No assumption as to "straightness" is ever assumed; therefore, the ordering of such observed changes in position is defined as of some curvature, and that either constant or not-constant, but regular.

The principled notion, that man's increase of power in the universe is orderable, is defined in respect to the "clock" provided by regular curvature in astronomical processes. This is also the "clock" used for transoceanic navigation.

The fact that man can increase his power, per capita, and per square kilometer, as measured by such "clocks," by discovery of added universal physical principles, is the prime axiom on which the foundations of Classical artistic composition are lain. This is defined as the correlation between such changes in knowledge for practice, and the increase of mankind's power, per capita, and per square kilometer of the Earth's surface.

This becomes the prime axiom of Classical-artistic principle, the definition of the individual nature of man and woman, as absolutely distinct from, and absolutely above the beasts. This prime axiom thus defines human forms of individual behavior, as distinct from the merely animal-like behavior which can be, and often is imitated by persons.

2. The Cognitive Axiom.

The instant we focus upon that process, by means of which validatable universal discoveries of principle are generated, we encounter a second barrier. This barrier is associated with the cognitive axiom.

All discoveries of principle are generated, by individual minds confronted with the evidence of those kinds of errors in existing belief, for which there are no deductive solutions. These unique predicaments are called *ontological paradoxes* in scientific work,[25] and are usually identified as *metaphors* within the domain of Classical forms of artistic composition. The two terms mean the same thing; the distinction in use of the terms, is that the one refers to the peculiarities of discovery of universal physical principle, the second to the peculiarities of generating a discovery of universal Classical-artistic, or analogous principle.

In science, such ontological paradoxes arise in the form of undeniable evidence which violates the doctrines of existing knowledge. If this evidence is of the form which defies any possible solution within the scope of deductive methods, it is to be recognized as a true *ontological paradox*. In such cases, validatable solutions are generated by those sovereign synthetic actions of individual minds which Immanuel Kant denied to exist, and are generated only in this way. The generation of such validatable forms of synthetic solutions is called *cognition*.

After such a discovery of universal physical principle is made, the solution can be proven by those methods which are associated with the notion of a *unique experiment*, a design of experiment cohering with Riemann's notion of a multiply-connected manifold. However, the discovery, once proven, can be known by a second person, only if and when that second person has repeated the cognitive experience of the first person. *This is the universal principle of cognition.* This principle, so defined, supplies the meaning of the terms "knowing" and "knowledge." It is validatable ideas (principles) generated by means of replicatable synthetic acts of cognition, which constitute the elements of the body of knowledge, as contrasted with mere opinion, the latter including merely learned opinion.

I must emphasize, that although the validated discoveries of universal principle produced by cognition, are products of the mind, rather than sense-perception as such, since their validation depends upon experimental validation, the adoption of such synthesized principles depends absolutely upon the demonstration of the efficiency of such principles in effecting a qualitative increase in mankind's power in and over the universe. Thus, all such principled ideas are securely

---

25. They are sometimes referred to as "crucial paradoxes," for which solutions are associated with the relatively commonplace use of the term "crucial experiments." Normally, I do not use the term "crucial experiments," because the term is associated with a relatively sloppy way of thinking about the method for proving universal physical principles. I prefer the definition of *unique experiment*, as associated with Riemann's 1854 habilitation dissertation.

rooted in man's efficient relationship to the universe. Thus, they are never "merely ideas," but are true, experimentally validated universal principles.

Thus, this principle of experimentally validated cognition is also a universal principle. It is this principle of cognition, so defined, which, in turn, defines the *active principle of individual human nature*, and that axiomatically.

3. The Classical artistic principle.

If two, or more persons, have shared the experience of generating the same, validatable universal principle by means of individual cognition, each is capable, as Immanuel Kant and his followers could not, of *recognizing* the act of discovery which has been generated within the cognitive processes of the other.

In such cases, we have touched a faculty of experience which lies outside mere sense-perception. Now, we have, in addition to those images associated with sense-perception, another set of images associated with *recognizable cognition*. These ideas are linked to physical reality through relevant forms of experimental validation. All ideas, whether scientific, or artistic ideas, or Platonic ideas of natural law[26] and politics, belong to this category of conceptions generated by recognizable cognition, rather than mere sense-perception. This is the definition of what are termed *Platonic Ideas*, in opposition to mere opinions.

The fact that shared knowledge of validated discoveries of universal principles depends absolutely on this interactive relationship among the cognitive processes of individual persons, defines the axiomatic principle underlying the notion of the distinctively human quality of *social relations*.[27]

This axiomatic quality of human social relations, when addressed as social relations, defines the meaning of Classical artistic composition. The essential quality implied in such artistic composition is the Socratic quality of *truthfulness*, as Plato puts these notions of truthfulness and justice in the mouth of Socrates, as contrasted with the intrinsically untruthful opinions of the opposing characters Thrasymachus and Glaucon. This quality of truthfulness lies in reliance upon the peculiarly Socratic notion of validatable products of cognitive synthesis.

That much said, now focus upon the role of Classical artistic composition in defining the universal principles which apply to the proper ordering of social relations generally.

For purposes of education in classrooms, the best illustration of what is meant by ideas (i.e., Platonic Ideas), is the contrast between the model of Classical sculpture, as typified by the model cases of Scopas and Praxiteles, in contrast to the relative deadness of not only pre-Classical Greek and Egyptian "Archaic" sculpture, and also the decadent forms of Roman sculpture. Notable is the decadence of Roman efforts to imitate Classical Greek sculpture. This work of Scopas and Praxiteles must be compared with the paintings of Leonardo da Vinci, Raphael Sanzio, and Rembrandt. Leonardo's mural, **The Last Supper**, is the best choice of pedagogical model of the connection between the Classical sculpture of Scopas and Praxiteles, and the revolutionary perspective which Leonardo introduced to painting.

The characteristic of Classical sculpture is that it is apparently "off balance." In fact, the mind perceives this as a piece of static marble which conveys to the mind of the observer the notion of a body in mid-motion. Not anything "off balance" will produce this effect; it must register in the mind as a truthful image of a body in its proper mid-motion. This occurs in the mind in the same way that cognition functions to generate the notion of a true Idea.

The same principle underlies the methods of Classical musical composition of J.S. Bach, and such Bach followers as Mozart, Hadyn, Beethoven, and Brahms, in contrast and opposition to the virtually idea-free banality of the French decadent, Romantic composer Rameau. As Bach's **A Musical Offering** and his posthumously published **The Art of the Fugue** illustrate the connection, it is Bach's use of the principle of inversion, within a context of Florentine *bel canto* polyphony, which generates the principle of well-tempering, and the methods which, beginning with Mozart's compositions of the early 1780s, launched the method of Classical thorough-composition also associated with the subsequent compositions of Haydn, Beethoven, Schubert, Mendelssohn, Schumann, and Brahms.

In Classical musical composition, the use of the principle of inversion to generate, and to resolve lawful

---

26. e.g., constitutional law.

27. The quality of *loving*, as identified in the writings of Plato and the Apostle Paul by the Greek term *agapē*, is a quality which exists only within the domain of cognitive social relations, not sense-perception. One loves a person not because "they are beautiful to look at," but because the cognitive interaction with them is beautiful, because they have beautiful souls. This is the meaning of the term "beauty" as applicable to Classical artistic compositions, and to the passion for truth and justice, in opposition to the evil which is the Lockean or other notion of purely positive law.

dissonances, and their resolution, in a polyphonic mode, produce compositions which in and of themselves represent true ideas, in the sense of Platonic Ideas.

The lawful resolutions of these successive dissonances, impart to the entire composition a sense of subsuming *motion*, of cognitive "energy," to an effect akin to the sense of the idea of motion evoked by a Classical Greek sculpture. It is the musical performer's (and conductor's) ability to evoke the idea of that contrapuntal

---

The most notable of the general follies which have defined the predictable course of the recent thirty-odd years of U.S. history, is the disengagement of the mind of the victim, the typical citizen, from his, or her former sense of an efficient connection between his existence, and the physical reality of the economy upon which individual existence depends.

---

motion, rather than a mere succession of transitions, from the performance, which produces the effect which the century's greatest conductor, Wilhelm Furtwängler, sometimes described as "performing between the notes."[28]

In the case of Classical thorough-composition, the power of the Classical medium lies in such exploitation of the medium of polyphony. Polyphony is premised upon Leonardo da Vinci's view of the characteristics of

---

28. The irreducible element of Classical musical composition, is the *polyphonic interval*, and not a mere interval between two successive tones of the scale. For example, when singing an interval, the mind must hear the inversion of that interval (for example). It is the dissonance generated, as in Classical thorough-composition, by the polyphonic antiphony of "parallel" intervals, which defines the polyphonic, as distinct from the ordinary, relatively linear sung interval of an individual voice. Hence, a minimum of a third tone must be added to each interval and its inversion, to bring the mind to focus on the metaphor located elementally within the simple unit of Classical musical composition. Hence, musicians must think in terms of well-tempering, rather than equal tempering. The singer (and Classical composer) uses the natural voice qualities of registration and coloration to reflect the polyphonic principle within the sung part. The polyphonic interval is not heard in the ear, but in the mind, in the same way, on principle, that the perception of motion in a static piece of Classical sculpture, defines the idea of the latter sculpture as something existing only in the domain of cognition, rather than mere sense-perception. Thus, well-tempering is Classical, whereas equal tempering is Archaic on principle. Hence, for Furtwängler, "performing between the notes."

the six distinct singing-voice species, natural to the human singing voice's best potentials. The participation of several, or all among these singing-voice species, and the addition of instruments designed and performed to imitate the *bel canto* characteristics of the relevant singing-voice imitated, gives to such Classical thorough-composition a unique power as an expression of social relations in the performance of Classical art-forms.

In the medium of Classical tragedy, as marked by the tragedies of Aeschylus, Sophocles, Shakespeare, and Schiller, we have the most direct connection between Classical artistic composition and political principles. It is that connection, and its practical implications for today, on which I focus, in defining the role of forecasting in defining a recovery program for the present U.S. situation.

Today's U.S.A. as a Classical Tragedy

Shakespeare's **Hamlet** is, for various reasons, the most easily recognized demonstration of the relevance of Classical tragedy for defining the proper principles of political life generally. The essence of the matter is summarized by comparing the famous Third Act soliloquy, along with the ultimate outcome of the decision which Hamlet presents there, to the situation in the final scene of the play as a whole.

Essentially, Hamlet refuses to change his ways, even after he has recognized that the decision perhaps dooms him and his nation. In the final act, with Hamlet and other relevant characters dead on stage, Shakespeare puts into the motion of a surviving character, the injunction, as if to the audience: Let us learn the lessons of the bloody outcome we have just witnessed, while the experience is fresh in our minds.

All of the great Classical tragedies, from Aeschylus and Sophocles, through Shakespeare and Schiller, have the utmost relative, sometimes even absolute validity, as demonstrations of universal political principle. A similar, and related importance, is to be found in such other expressions of the Commedia art as Bocaccio's **Decameron**, the **Gargantua** and **Pantagruel** of François Rabelais, Cervantes' **Don Quixote**, and Swift's **Gulliver's Travels**. Blood and ridicule, if either were well composed, may induce the cognitive processes of audiences to recognize, as a matter of principle, the penalties of certain kinds of folly.

The most notable of the general follies which have defined the predictable course of the recent thirty-odd years of U.S. history, is the disengagement of the mind of the victim, the typical citizen, from his, or her former sense of an efficient connection between his existence, and the physical reality of the economy upon which individual existence depends. This specific form of personal moral perversion was already rampant in English-speaking history, in the legacies of Thomas Hobbes and John Locke, and also in the radically irrationalist notion of the "invisible hand" adopted by the cult-followers of Bernard Mandeville and Adam Smith.

The form in which this erupted as a mass phenomenon in the U.S.A., during the 1964-1972 interval, owes its most significant proximate origins to the poisonous irrationalism of the German and French existentialists of the 1920s and 1930s, as typified by Martin Heidegger, Hannah Arendt, and Theodor Adorno for Germany, and Nazi philosopher Heidegger's clone Jean-Paul Sartre (and Frantz Fanon) for France.[29]

As Heidegger intimate Hannah Arendt emphasized, the root of the existentialism represented in common by herself, Heidegger, Jaspers, Adorno, and Sartre, is the radical irrationalism of Immanuel Kant: Kant's, and post-Kantian philosophical liberalism's denial of the knowable existence of truth. In effect, Arendt's most famous treatise paints herself as a kind of Gaea, a virtual consort of Python-Satan, and, in her own right, the "mother of lies." This existentialism, as purveyed in the U.S.A. by the Josiah Macy, Jr. Foundation's circles of Bertrand Russell, Margaret Mead, Gregory Bateson, Norbert Wiener, et al., formed the crucial point of reference for what became the "rock-drug-sex youth-counterculture" of the 1964-1972 university campus.

The essential significance of these expressions of existentialist irrationalism for the predictability of the post-1960s U.S. population's trends in opinion, is that these mass developments, initially centered in the university student populations of the 1964-1972 interval, became "a march through the institutions," a virtual locust-plague of irrationalism, whose spreading influence prompted more and more among the general population, especially the younger generations, to make an open break with reason itself. The characteristic of this

29. The corrupting influences of the phenomenology of Husserl, and the neo-Kantian Karl Jaspers, are notable influences upon the development of the German existentialist followers of the satanist Friedrich Nietzsche.

increasingly lunatic trend, was a militant aversion to the suggestion that there must be some efficient connection between the material means for producing human existence, and the goals of human existence.

In summation, a break with the notion that opinions ought to be based upon validatable principles respecting mankind's relationship to the universe in general. Hence, especially after the effects of the 1979-1982 phase of Federal Reserve Chairman Volcker's rampaging destruction of the U.S.'s real economy, the trend in

---

Cut loose from earlier, traditional moorings to sanity, the post-1964-1972 population lost its moorings within the real universe. Reality ceased to be a standard for judging which opinions were sane, and which not.

---

shaping of popular opinion became more and more insane—literally insane.

Typical of this process, was the increase in the ration of the labor-force employed in those forms of "services" which are of doubtful value to the real economy and the real population, an increase coinciding with a collapse in the percentile of the labor-force employed in useful forms of employment. The break from the idea of producing, or assisting the production of useful physical goods, contributed to fostering a sense of a break away from a rational sense of the means by which a population acquires its income, from the production of the wealth on which that income depends. The man-to-nature relationship become more and more distant, even broken psychologically, in this way. Thus, the protective link to personal sanity was strained to the utmost, even broken in the manner the brutish Mark Barton episode illustrates.

Cut loose, thus, from earlier, traditional moorings to sanity, the post-1964-1972 population lost its moorings within the real universe. Reality ceased to be a standard for judging which opinions were sane, and which not.

The worst part of this, was not that psychological break with reality, which dominates the majority among "baby boomers," x's, and y's today. The worst part, has been the passion with which these errant minds defend those opinions and preferences which impel them to reject the physical reality of human existence, just because physical reality is seen as an alien force whose influence they must resist, even reject. Thus, they have an impassioned impulse to take pleasure from savaging those ideas which suggest submission of the mind to the validation of the principles of social practice with the real, physical universe.

This leads our attention to an additional, axiomatic principle of Classical artistic composition.

What Makes the Clock Tick?

In earlier published locations, I have emphasized my agreement with Friedrich Schiller on the subject of the contrast between the way in which animals and

---

What is the passion which pushes the thinker to reaching the cognitive solution, to holding like a terrier to the moral issue, until, finally, a truthful solution is discovered? Plato's Socrates, like the Apostle Paul, answered: Agapē.

---

people play. This connection is aptly illustrated by such cases as the child and puppy playing happily together, or observing the relationship between man and horse in dressage. In both cases, a certain point of similarity, but also, contrary to the impassioned belief of Britain's avowedly bestial Prince Philip, an absolute, principled difference, between man and beast, is demonstrated.

The happy puppy or horse at play displays a certain outward similarity to the happy child. The difference is, the child's most intense expression of happiness at play arises from the child's successful cognitive experience, of making a discovery of principle, which is, for that child, an original such discovery. This is complemented by the fact, that when the adult ceases to show the quality of happy play in attacking ontological paradoxes, or has no happy sense of metaphor, that adult is showing us that he, or she has gone creatively stale, as psychiatrist Dr. Lawrence Kubie described cases of neurotic distortion of the creative process.

The issue immediately under scrutiny at this moment, is, "What makes the clock tick?" We have pointed to certain characteristics of the cognitive process. What is the driving force which sets those characteristics into motion? What is the passion which pushes the thinker to reaching the cognitive solution, to holding like a terrier to the moral issue, until, finally, a truthful solution is discovered? Plato's Socrates, like the Apostle Paul, answered: *Agapē*.

There remains, despite the qualitative distinction, something to be learned from the happy puppy at play. In the beast, as in the person, we observe something important in common, something we might wish to name as "a zest for living." This, the happy person and happy beast share, at play. Yet, since this zest for living is a matter of expressing one's nature, there is a corresponding difference in the result. In short, the truly human person makes cognitive discoveries, not for profit, but because it is the natural expression of happiness to do so.

The added difference is, that while the beast, even the chimpanzee, can learn from experience, no beast can transmit cognitive discoveries of universal principle from one person, or one generation, to another. Thus, while the beast has a biological connection to its species as a whole, the pet's personality lives on only through participating in the life of the human beings associated with it. Only mankind affords its individual person a cognitive, personal identity in all eternity, through the radiation of the original discovery of validatable universal principles, both physical principles and those principles typified by Classical artistic composition.

Here, in the latter connections, the individual's zest for life is expressed, a zest, which, in its best expression, is the individual person participating in his species through receiving and generating those ideas which meet the standard of universal principles. Such uniquely human, creative playfulness, is the distinction of the human form of zest for life. This is the mainspring of society's progress, the energy which makes the clock tick.

When this form of the zest for life is at full tilt, we witness the creative personality optimistically at work. It feels like play, but it is the motor-force of all human progress at work. On the contrary, when cultural pessimism takes over, the crabby personality tends to behave as a Hobbes or Locke might propose, even to the degree of becoming what the Twentieth Century would recognize as the fascist beast-man of the type of Martin Heidegger, Hannah Arendt, et al.

Thus, in forecasting the direction in which the outcome of current history will be shaped, we must consider both the axiomatic characteristics of policy-shaping, and also the interrelationship of that with the contrasting qualities of cultural pessimism, or optimism.

The tendency has been, that when a combination of

alienation from reality coincides with a self-feeding process of increasing intense cultural pessimism, the very worst destiny tends to be the virtually inevitable outcome of the relevant part of current history. On this account, periods of cultural decadence, such as those of the 1964-1972 interval to present date, tend to go to their limit. That limit is usually defined by a form of collapse of that society, a form consistent with the characteristic flaws of that society as an unfolding, degenerative process. This is what we, in the U.S.A. and much of the rest of the world, have experienced as an unfolding process, during the recent decades.

When the force of reality has shattered what had been the force of social authority attributed to the decaying regime, the society has a chance to recover. In such moments of crisis, the controlling delusions of earlier time are discredited. Reality stalks forth. If the society accepts reality, it may recover, and even learn from that experience, not to repeat such follies in the future.

That is the principle which every great Classical tragedy has taught its audience. It is from real-life tragedy, as the Classical stage brings that into focus for its audience, that societies may not merely revive, but rise to higher levels than ever before. All Classical artistic composition has a similar function. All that we know of man's nature, in this respect, we learn through the medium of Classical artistic composition.

3. Epilogue: Crisis and Mind-set

What, then, defines the outer limits of existence of a form of society self-governed by a tragically fatal sort of mind-set?

The general answer is already implied by the bare notion of a Gauss-Riemann manifold. In this instance, the manifold is of the LaRouche-Riemann form, as the interrelationship of universal physical and Classical-artistic principles has been identified here. Summed up in the fewest possible words: all such systems are self-bounded systems, in the same general sense that a sphere is a self-bounded system throughout.

The more specific analogy, is the case of a planetary orbit, as the Kepler-Leibniz-Gauss-Riemann notion of regular non-constant curvature defines a regular orbit, or any other manifold of this type. In such cases, or any analogous one, the limits of the system are self-bounded, as the analogy of the sphere suggests.

The U.S. economy and associated Bretton Woods system, as these have coexisted since the 1971 introduction of the ultimately self-doomed "floating exchange-rate monetary system," are an inherently self-doomed system, which, if their existence is continued in that form, must converge on a certain boundary-state, at which they must, in effect, be turned inward upon themselves, and destroy themselves in that way.

The key to understanding that system, in particular, is to place emphasis upon the vicious discrepancy between the characteristic form of action which is built into the system, axiomatically, and the real universe on which the system acts, the universe also acting upon the system.

My Triple-Curve illustration is the simplest possible representation of the way in which that tragic self-boundedness of the presently doomed system has been defined. The flight from reality, upon which the system has been based, since the 1964-1972 cultural-paradigm shift, has been into a "post-industrial fantasy life," but a fantasy-life whose physical continuation depends upon the very real economy from which the fantasy-life is fleeing, and attempting to destroy all at once. The resulting, geometrically increasing discrepancy between that fantasy and the rejected reality on which the fantasy's continuation depends, defines a limit, exactly as my Triple Curve simply defines the essential relations among the fantasy and the economic reality.

In such a situation, no matter what tricks are used, in the effort to perpetuate the doomed illusion, the more the tricks, the more inevitable the doom. When the rate of pressures from the real economy, against the fantasy-system, are increased more by the tricks, than the gains won by the tricks themselves, the system has reached its outer limit of continued existence. That illustrates the notion of a self-bounded system. That defines where the world is at this time.

Under such conditions, the question of survival becomes, simply, can enough people be prompted to make the necessary changes in their axiomatic assumptions, fast enough, in time, to set into motion the new, viable economic process, which is required if mankind is to be prevented from going to its doom along with the inevitably doomed, tragic old system now collapsing. The question is, can you organize your neighbor to awaken, and become sane again, in time to launch the new system, before we all go down together for failure to launch the new system in a timely fashion?

Give Economic Development a Chance

by Rachel Brown

May 8—Despite the barrage of political warfare from the mainstream media attempting to divide the nation into discreet "political wings" perpetually alienated by "hot-button single issues," there is agreement on profound common principles among the vast majority of all people. Simultaneously, there is a clear intention for, and movement toward progress in regard to certain fundamental aspects of those principles by the current Presidency. In truth, the principles of Lyndon LaRouche's "Four New Laws" define the essential policy direction around which the nation can be unified, and these laws, though not yet fully understood, have not been ignored.

Manuel Tilca

LaRouche PAC organizer Daniel Burke talking to participants at the April 29, 2017 address by President Trump in Harrisburg, Pennsylvania.

I met in Cincinnati with Republican small-business owners who are still hurting from the bursting of the housing bubble and the bailout of Wall Street. "Why didn't underwater homeowners get any help?" one of them asked rhetorically. "Because Wall Street has all the power." Others nodded in agreement.

In Raleigh, I heard from local bankers who thought Bill Clinton should never have repealed the Glass-Steagall Act. "Clinton was in the pockets of Wall Street just like George W. Bush was," said one.

Most are also dead-set against the Trans-Pacific Partnership. In fact, they're opposed to trade agreements, including NAFTA, that they believe have made it easier for corporations to outsource American jobs abroad.

The common aims of these diverse "political categories" were illustrated by "liberal Democrat" Robert Reich in his "Red State Tour" of November 2015. He explained it as follows. "I've just returned from three weeks in 'red' America. It was ostensibly a book tour, but I wanted to talk with conservative Republicans and Tea Partiers. I intended to put into practice what I tell my students—that the best way to learn, is to talk with people who disagree with you. I wanted to learn from red America, and hoped they'd also learn a bit from me (and perhaps also buy my book). But something odd happened. It turned out that many of the conservative Republicans and Tea Partiers I met agreed with much of what I had to say, and I agreed with them."

He went on to elaborate:

President Trump also addressed a number of these core principles in his April 30 address in Pennsylvania, where he avoided the "dishonest media" and spoke directly to the American people, defining his primary policy objectives and initiatives:

For decades our country has lived through the greatest job theft in the history of the world. Our factories were shuttered, our steel mills closed down, and our jobs were stolen away and shipped far away to other countries, some of which you've never even heard of.

To protect our jobs and our economic freedom, I immediately withdrew the United States from the horrible disaster that would have been another NAFTA but worse, the Trans-Pacific Partnership … the TPP would have been a tremendous disaster for our country, and we are not going to surrender Pennsylvania jobs ever again. We've done that once before—it's not going to happen.

We are reviewing every single trade deal, and wherever there is cheating, we will take immediate action and there will be a penalty. And we will renegotiate NAFTA, and if we don't get a good deal and a fair deal for our country … We'll start a renegotiation, and hopefully it will be fair for everybody, and if it's not a fair deal for our country—because you have to understand, we have been on the wrong side of the NAFTA deal for many, many years, many decades. We can't allow it to happen. So we are going to renegotiate, and if we can't make a fair deal for our companies and our workers, we will terminate NAFTA. . . .

I followed through on my promise and issued a new directive to buy American and hire American. In just these first few months, we created 99,000 new construction jobs, 49,000 new manufacturing jobs, and 27,000 new mining jobs. . . .

Although these initiatives don't meet the measure of LaRouche's complete economic program, the intention to revive the physical base of the U.S. economy is clear. The first of LaRouche's "Four Laws," Glass-Steagall, was also addressed by President Trump in an interview in the Oval Office on May 1st, when the President was asked, "Should we break up the big banks? Do you support that?" Trump responded, "There are—you know, some people that want to go back to the old system, right? So we're going to look at that. We're going to—we're looking at it right now as we speak."

Glass-Steagall is and always has been the only way to protect the real economy from the usurious nature of the "financial industry" run by Wall Street and London interests.

The LaRouche economic program involves extending the New Silk Road process of Eurasia into a World Landbridge infrastructure plan, and cooperating closely with China to carry it out. President Trump has ex-pressed the importance with which he regards the relationship with China, calling China's President Xi Jinping, "a man that I've gotten to like and respect," and stressing the common economic interests of the United States and China.

Secretary of State Rex Tillerson also expressed the President's objective of a new era of U.S.-China relations in an April 3 speech to the State Department.

Well, it's extraordinarily important—first to just the broader relationship of where U.S.-China relations are going to find themselves over the next two to three to four decades. I think we are at a bit of an inflection point in the U.S.-China relationship. Now, North Korea is a threat that presents itself right up front to both of us, and in our conversations with the Chinese—and we have been very clear to them—I was on my initial trips to Beijing and then in the visit of President Xi to Mar-a-Lago, the President and I were able to be very clear to them—that things have to change in North Korea and we need their help doing that.

I think we need to understand one another, and understand that China is on a pathway of continuing to emerge with their own people in terms of providing a quality of life to their own population. They've made enormous progress over the last 10 to 15 years—500 million Chinese have moved out of poverty into middle-class status.

Our understanding of them—and I think they need to have an understanding of us—is that we do not seek to constrain their need to continue their economic growth and to continue to help their people enjoy a better quality of life. As they are pursuing that, though, they have to do that in a way that supports stability around the rest of the world as well.

If the press were to report these facts, the American people would stop being manipulated around artificial biases, and instead would see the potential for dramatic change for the improvement of the entire nation, and for a new global paradigm. This will not be achieved by slapping together solutions for media-manufactured "issues," but by putting into motion a process which will emerge as a superior mode of human existence over the next 50 years.

WILLIAM BINNEY

'We Are Watching Our Democracy Go Down the Drain'

Jason Ross of the LaRouche PAC Science Team interviewed William Binney on May 5.

Jason Ross: Hi, I'm Jason Ross, and I'm very happy to be interviewing William Binney, a former senior National Security Agency (NSA) official. Mr. Binney served in the NSA for more than 30 years, including as technical director of its World Geopolitical and Military Analysis Reporting Group. He worked on developing many of the technologies still used by the NSA, and he resigned in 2001 over the potential for a totalitarian, as he put it, Orwellian state, in which the technical means to spy on every American were being developed.

Let me ask you: Ever since Donald Trump won the Presidential election, there has been a drumbeat of attacks, stating that Russia threw the election to Trump, by hacking and releasing emails, by hiring Internet trolls, by collecting blackmail material, and other means. These claims have come from political circles, intelligence circles, former British MI6 agent Christopher Steele, and others.

Let me ask you, Mr. Binney: What do you think about these claims? Did Russian hackers elect Donald Trump?

William Binney: I wrote an article that was published in *Consortiumnews* on Dec. 12th of last year that said this was all a big fabrication, simply because they weren't saying exactly where the hack came from and where the data out of the hack went to. That's the whole point of what NSA has set up, in terms of copying and collecting everything in a fiber network inside the United States, and virtually everything in the world on those fibers.

That means—and they've got trace route programs by the hundreds, scattered all over the world—that means that they can follow the [data] packets as they move through the net-

work. Now, if somebody hacks into the DNC [Democratic National Committee] or Hillary [Clinton's] or [former Clinton campaign chairman John] Podesta's email or something, and they want to find out who it is, all they have to do is use the IP address with XKeyscore, as Edward Snowden said, and they've got all the data to find out where the packets went. But they haven't done that. Even NSA, which is the only agency that can do this—the rest of them are meaningless—if NSA says they've got data on it, then it's meaningful. If the rest say that we have "high confidence," that's just pure

Miquel Taverna/CCCB

William Binney

speculation, that's just pure garbage, that doesn't mean anything. Produce the evidence! They haven't produced any at all. So that's what I called it back in December of last year.

Ross: More recently, about a little over a month ago, you co-authored an article with Ray McGovern in which you wrote about Trump's response to this, that "his choice may decide whether there is a future for this constitutional republic. Either Trump can acquiesce to or fight against a deep state of intelligence officials who have a myriad of ways to spy on politicians and other citizens, and thus amass derogatory materials that can be easily transformed into blackmail."

That's a strong claim. Tell us, how do you see the Trump response to this attack on elected government? And what should ordinary people do, to prevent such a policy coup?

Binney: First of all, I think President Trump realizes what's been going on. A recent statement he made about, "there's an awful lot of spying going on [against] U.S. citizens, and we really don't know the extent of it, and we really have to find out what the heck"—he used the word "hell"—"what the hell is going on." Well, that means they're even keeping him in the dark.

Now, as the President of the United States, he's supposed to know all the sources of information that the intelligence community is using to produce intelligence for him, and he obviously doesn't know about this. But I've made it perfectly clear that the "Fairview" program, "Stormbrew" programs, and "Blarney" programs for the tapping of fiber networks inside the United States are their sources of information on everybody in the United States, including representatives in the House and Senate; you know, even judges on the Supreme Court, Generals on the Joint Chiefs of Staff, all Federal judges, all senior lawyers in law firms all around, and all the journalists and everything; all that stuff is being captured and stored.

And what they're not talking about is—I've seen some arguments where they said, "Well, as long as we're only using it for intelligence, and law enforcement isn't involved, you know, it's okay for us to do that." That was the argument I think that Judge Napolitano put forward, that they were using with the FISA [Foreign Intelligence Surveillance Act] Court to dupe them into doing what they want.

U.S. Air Force photo/Staff Sgt. Jonathan Lovelady

U.S. Army Lt. General Michael Flynn testifying when he was director of the Defense Intelligence Agency, Feb. 4, 2014.

And that's really what's happened. They've been duped, and so have the Congress, most of Congress. The intelligence committees, I think, were more aware of what was going on than the rest of Congress. But they duped the rest of Congress! They made them all just play along like a bunch of sheep—"here's the bell, follow the bell." So, our democracy basically doesn't really exist the way it was originally intended. And the law enforcement—FBI, DEA, and others in the law enforcement community, had direct access into the NSA data, they've had it all along! Director [Robert] Mueller at the FBI said he'd been using the Stellar Wind, which is the domestic spying data, since 2001, he'd been using that, and that's direct access through their technology data center in Quantico, Virginia into the NSA databases where they could look at all the content and metadata of everybody in the country. And they could retroactively research them any time they want.

And they're using it to arrest people for common crimes inside the United States. So this is simply a destruction of the entire judicial process in our country, and it's a fundamental violation of constitutional rights. They've scrapped the Constitution, fundamentally.

That's why, when the Iraqis were struggling to put together a Constitution, I said, "Well, why don't we give them ours? We're not using it."

Ross: One specific example of that recently is [former DIA and former National Security Council Director] Michael Flynn, who, his conversations with a

Russian diplomat were recorded, which happens, but then the unmasking—it was reported that was done by Susan Rice, Obama's National Security Advisor. As you put it, this sounds just like what J. Edgar Hoover used the FBI to do: collecting blackmail material to exert political control. What must be done to prevent such control, such blackmail potential through agents operating through the intelligence sector? What do we do about this?

Binney: You have to have some Attorney General who will take action to stop this. This is a violation of the fundamentals of the Constitution and the Bill of Rights, and also a violation of the existing law. They tried—like in 2008 when Congress passed a retroactive immunity for the telecommunications companies. That was because these companies were giving them access to the fiber lines, and letting them take all the data off the fiber lines, and because they were also giving them all the data on all their customers. It was trying to retroactively give immunity to people who were committing an unconstitutional act—which is unconstitutional and therefore not a law.

That's why I'm supporting four separate attempts to challenge that in federal court. We're challenging them based on the constitutionality of what the NSA is collecting. Once that challenge gets up, and gets into the Supreme Court—it's obvious that it's unconstitutional, any idiot can see that. What that means is that once it's declared unconstitutional, their whole house of cards falls. All those laws they tried to pass to protect people also fall, because they are not constitutional. You can't authorize an unconstitu-

CC/George Rex

Sign in Britain referring to the UK's Government Communications Headquarters.

tional act with a law. That law is not a law, because it doesn't conform to the Constitution.

So, these are the things I am trying to do. I think everybody should challenge them in federal court, but also the political way to do it is you need to fire people on the intelligence committees, because they are advocates for this kind of crap. They are also part and parcel of covering up what they are really doing to the rest of Congress. You need to focus on them, and also in the courts, and get the courts to recognize what's really been going on. They are so afraid of doing anything when it comes to national security, because it's such an unfamiliar topic to them. But the Constitution is not an unfamiliar topic. All they have to do is pay attention to that and rule based on that. That's the simple answer.

The British Police State

Ross: On the international side of this, according to recent reports, some of the initial launching of these investigations into Trump were sparked by interventions from the UK, as were the totally deranged reports coming from MI6 agent Christopher Steele, including salacious claims about Trump's behavior. Under the "Five Eyes" arrangement a lot of intelligence sharing occurs between the NSA and, for example, the UK's GCHQ [Government Communications Headquarters].

Let me ask, is having a foreign country with an unsavory and imperial history being so tightly tied to our intelligence services—is this a concern for you? How do you see this international partnership?

Binney: I think it's gotten a little too involved, in my view anyway. For example, other than the

"FIVE EYES" NATIONS

Aerial view of the GCHQ in Cheltenham, Gloucestershire.

defenceimages.mod.uk

they've got a large access to the transoceanic cables going from Europe to America through Bude [in Cornwall] and a couple of other places too. That gives them a lot more than that. The British part of it is just bad enough for them, but also they're getting all the records on U.S. citizens that are routed through any of the access points that they've got. I think it's really a situation that needs some effective monitoring. The oversight we have now with the FISA court and the intelligence committees is a farce, it's a joke. They don't do anything; they can't achieve anything and they can't verify anything they're being told by the intelligence agencies. So it's really a sham, it's a charade.

Ross: This might be asking you to speculate, but you had mentioned how there is a potential for spying on federal officials, judges, top level political layers inside the United States. The intelligence committees themselves I would imagine would be a prime target for this sort of compromising type of control. Do you think that is a factor in the cowardice being shown by the intelligence committees?

Binney: Yes, that's part of it, because even when Senator [Chuck] Schumer [D-NY] warned President Trump that he shouldn't go after the intelligence community because they've got many ways to get back at him, well, this is exactly one of them. What that's really saying is that everything they've done electronically has also been captured, and they can go back and look at everything they're doing, and everything they've ever done for the past 10 or 15 years. That's definitely it. We had another whistleblower, Russell Tice, who had made it perfectly clear that this is the kind of activity that is going on. He even said that in some of the areas he was, where he saw this data, he saw the transcripts of phone calls of the then-Senator Obama.

I've been calling it the imperial guard—for the Roman Empire their imperial guard basically determined who the emperors were and what they did. That's what is happening here with the intelligence community.

law enforcement and now other intelligence agencies that Obama had opened up the NSA data to, the people with direct access to the NSA database are the "Five Eyes" countries [United States, Canada, New Zealand, Britain, and Australia]. GCHQ has had it since 2007 at least, and the others were following that probably in 2008 or 2009. So that means that they can go in directly into the database too. And when you do that, you can actually pick and put in place and select the kinds of information you want and ignore the rest.

In other words, if there is exculpatory data in there about the Trump campaign program or anybody involved in it, they may simply be ignoring that, and only putting forward something that may indicate that they were involved, might indicate a suspicion or something. So it's a matter of selecting the data that you look at, instead of looking at the whole set of information to get an overall picture. That's one thing I don't trust them to do. First of all, they are even messing up their own country with their investigative powers bill. At least they openly admit they are going after everything everyone is doing on the web, and they are trying to get the companies, the Internet service providers, to provide it to them, and do a lot of work for them against everybody in the UK, as well, who are using the web and acquiring things on the web. They want them to create an Internet connection record, is what they call it. They were estimating about 60 billion records, Internet records, per day, for British citizens alone. But

Ross: Do you know if there was a lot of push-back or fight around the Five Eyes sharing, around giving access to such sensitive material to foreign governments?

Binney: I've never heard any opposition to that at all. Because fundamentally the Five Eyes are the ones that are doing this worldwide bulk data acquisition. They are the core of it. There are about eight or nine other countries around the world that are also participating, and they've got limited access to that data. But the core is the Five Eyes, and I believe they have almost unfettered access to it.

Ross: You had mentioned that you are pursuing lawsuits as a way of challenging these activities through federal courts. How are those proceeding?

Binney: They are still going, but the Government is trying to slow roll them because they know that when it comes to the Constitution and what they are doing, that they are actively performing unconstitutional activities, and they don't want it exposed in federal court or to the public because all of those activities are fundamentally impeachable offenses—that's what we impeached Richard Nixon for, violation of constitutional rights of U.S. citizens. That's exactly what's going on now, except now it's involving everybody. Back then Nixon could only handle a few thousand people. With the FBI, NSA, the CIA—all of them are doing it now. You had the CIA break into the Senate when they were writing that summary paper about the torture; you had them break into their servers. They got caught at it anyway.

Ross: And didn't exactly receive much punishment for such a brazen act.

Binney: Well what can you do when people have the goods on you? Who is going to do anything against them?

Spying and Blackmail

Ross: This is something that people have to be aware of, understanding the potential of the use of blackmail, and certain agencies that are collecting the material for it. That makes it possible, I suppose, to inoculate or immunize against the effects of being able to bring out a scandal on demand, if people are aware that's used as a political technique and its origins.

Eliot Spitzer, former New York Governor and prosecutor.

Binney: Yes, and they use it internationally too, it's not just in the United States. They used this against Jim Rosen, the Associated Press, other reporters, the Tea Party, the Occupy group— anybody who is doing something that they don't particularly care for, they go after and try to get rid of them, like General [David] Petraeus, General [John] Allen, and also [former New York Governor] Eliot Spitzer. They went after Spitzer— he was going after the bankers for defrauding people. The problem is the way the banks were packaging the deals. They were forced by Congress to approve loans that couldn't be supported by people getting them. That made that a bad investment, so they had to package it. Then they sold these packages around the world, and they fraudulently advertised them. That's what Eliot Spitzer was going after them for, for fraudulently soliciting people to buy these packaged deals, and they had to stop that because it would lead back to the Congress of the United States. That would expose them, so they had to stop it. So they got rid of Eliot.

What was the probable cause for anybody to investigate Eliot Spitzer? I can't think of one except, "Oh, he's going after our bankers."

Ross: In the aftermath of the revelations of the spying on [Martin Luther] King, there was the Church Committee [chaired by Senator Frank Church (D-ID)], there was the efforts of Congressman Neil Gallagher [D-NJ]; this is when the intelligence committees were created. Was that an effective push-back at the time? What would something like that look like today?

Binney: I think fundamentally we need another Church Committee that is open to the public all the way, that isn't hidden, no closed sessions at all, especially when it comes to exposing violations of our constitutional rights and the rights of people, period. I think that this needs to be out in the open and those who are doing it should be held accountable in the open. If it comes to indicting them, I think that that is a proper way to do things, that they need to be indicted, and the law should be adhered to—in my view anyway.

Schematic diagram of the NSA's Fairview surveillance program.

Ross: One more technical question before a summary. At the opening you had discussed how, if Russian hackers had really gotten these emails and released them, the NSA would have been able to find out about that given that the NSA sees all Internet traffic. Some people say, however, that Tor is something the NSA isn't able to unravel completely. Would that have provided a potential technical means to make it possible to hide the tracks, moving the data around?

Binney: No, I think they could have at least gotten some of the packets. That's one of the reasons they put all the trace route programs in hundreds of switches on the Internet around the world. That's because they are tracing all the packet routes to try to reconstruct Tor. That was one of the purposes of it.

Ross: Is there anything else that you would like to say to our listeners?

Binney: The law enforcement use of this data is just outright disgraceful, and I would also point out that [FBI Director James] Comey has known about all of this material and the use of it since at least the hospital visit in 2004 to [former Attorney General John] Ashcroft, when Ashcroft was in the hospital and Comey was acting Attorney General, and he [Comey], at that point, refused to renew the program. He's known about it since then. All this business of saying, "Well, the Trump Tower, there was no wiretap directed at the Trump Tower." That's correct. Wiretapping is basically obsolete. That *word* is obsolete. Everything now is surveillance, and it is constant surveillance of everything. All of that data is captured and stored. So it's not a question of wiretapping any more but of targeting in the database that's been captured. If somebody wanted to go after then-candidate Trump, they would have gone into that database with his signatures and to go after all the data about him. That's targeting—once you've captured the data. Wiretapping is to get the data and capture it. The constant surveillance gets all that data anyway.

Ross: So there would be no need to have specific wiretapping of Trump, because everything is already collected?

Binney: That's right. It's a word game. Everything is a word game with these people now in the public. The public is being duped by this word game. That's all. And unless you know the ins and outs of what they do and how they do it, you think it sounds reasonable.

End of Constitutional Protections

Ross: It used to be that people were given the impression there was an absolute wall between intelligence gathering and criminal prosecution, where for example, there was a much lower bar for wiretap surveillance for national intelligence purposes. It seems like, from what you have been saying, that that barrier has been almost entirely eliminated. Is that true?

Binney: Yes, that's right, since 2001, according to FBI Director Mueller. He made that statement to Bart Gellman when Bart did an interview with him in 2011 for *Time* magazine. That's also on the web. The way he put it was we had been using the Stellar Wind program since 2001. You have to know what the Stellar Wind program is. That's the domestic spying data, the content and metadata of domestic spying. That's from the Fairview, Stormbrew, Blarney programs, where there are more than a hundred taps inside the United States are collecting all this data off the fiber network.

The Function of Intelligence Has Been Lost

Ross: You had proposed a different method of collection entirely, that you believe would have made it possible to safeguard privacy.

Binney: And also to succeed in stopping terrorism. Because now what they have is too much data altogether. They can't get through it in time to assess threats, so they can't stop the threats. People get killed, then they go clean up the mess. Then they go after the people they knew did it because they have lots of data already stored on them. From there on it's like forensics. Intelligence has become a forensics job, a police job, after the fact, after the crime, when in fact the purpose of intelligence is to predict intentions and capabilities of adversaries in advance so you can do something to stop it.

They've lost that entire perspective. We are paying tens of billions of dollars to capture everything (every year, by the way), and actually are not able to use it or do anything with it. That's the big swindle that we're all under now: We are doing this collection of *everything* for terrorism, and yet you can't do a thing to stop it because of all you've collected. Then a terrorist attack happens they say we need more data, more money, and more people. They are building an empire at the expense of the few people that have to die now and then, to keep the program going.

Ross: Do you see this as a funding or an allocation of resources issue? Also as a methodology problem, in terms of the approach that analysts are taking to the use of data that we do have?

Binney: It's basically a combination of all of that. Fundamentally the motivation of these agencies is to swindle the public out of money, to build a bigger empire, intelligence empire, contracting empire, and governmental empire. It takes a lot of people to do all of this collection, and a lot of contracts and a lot of contractors to be involved to make it happen. So that's an empire you build and it costs a lot of money to do it. I reckon they're spending $100 billion a year on the intelligence community, all 17 agencies. Whereas, if President Trump wants to build a wall, he can take $2 billion out of CIA and $2 billion out of the NSA program every year and they wouldn't miss it. It wouldn't affect them at all. They couldn't do any worse than they are doing right now anyway.

Ross: Is there anything else you would like to add to conclude?

Binney: No, except the law enforcement use of this data is corrupting our entire judicial process. It's really making a sham of it. I would add one case, "Amnesty International vs. Clapper," that made it all the way to the Supreme Court. When the Solicitor General of the United States argued the case of the Government against the Amnesty challenge—Amnesty charged that the Government was using data to criminally convict people without telling them the source of it, thus preventing any challenges under the discovery rules, as is their constitutional right in a court of law, to challenge any of the discovery material used against them in a court of law. But the Government couldn't confess openly that it all came from NSA because all of that data was acquired without a warrant that meant it would be thrown out, which meant that the Government had no case. So they had to do these parallel constructions, create the data, and use that as a substitute for the NSA data in a court of law. That's a violation of the principle of all the constitutional rights of citizens. And it really makes a sham of our entire judicial process. We are actually watching our democracy go right down the drain here.

Ross: Thank you very much. This is certainly a very sobering assessment. I think it's a good kick in the pants for people who aren't aware of this, and provides some opportunities, some avenues of what can be done about it. So, William Binney, thank you very much.

Binney: Well, thank you.

EDITORIALS

Our Mission to Future Mankind

by Diane Sare

Steer, courageous sailor! Although the wit may deride
*   you,*
And the skipper at th' helm lower his indolent hand—
Ever, ever to th' West! There must the coast be
*   appearing,*
Yet she lies clearly and lies shimm'ring before your
*   mind's eye.*
Trust in the guiding God and follow the silent ocean,
Were she not yet, she'd rise now from the billows aloft.
Genius stands with Nature in everlasting union,
What is promised by the one, surely the other fulfils.
                    —"Columbus" by Friederich Schiller,
                        translated by William Wertz

This poem was brought to mind during a conversation this past week with Schiller Institutes founder Helga Zepp-LaRouche. The topic was the challenge presented to organizers by fast breaking and often contradictory global developments—how does one keep up, and provide qualified leadership to a confused and demoralized population? Mrs. LaRouche responded that the priority must be to have in one's mind's eye an image of what the world should look like 50 or 150 years from now. She said then one must attack those things which would prevent this vision from coming into being, and support and build on those which contribute to its realization. Not coincidentally, her husband Lyndon LaRouche authored a book by the title, *The Earth's Next 50 Years*, over a decade ago which does exactly that, and more.

This past week, Secretary of State Rex Tillerson held a discussion with members of the U.S. State Department where he also expressed that his reference point is 50 years from now, and that the intent of the Trump Administration is to act with the next 50 years in mind. After 16 years of Bush and Obama, this was highly unusual, and probably the most competent speech on U.S. foreign policy made by any government official in the last 17 years. A few sections of this speech are excerpted below.

So let's talk first about my view of how you translate "America first" into our foreign policy. And I think I approach it, really, that it's America first for national security and economic prosperity, and that doesn't mean it comes at the expense of others.

Our partnerships and our alliances are critical to our success in both of those areas. But as we have progressed over the last 20 years—and some of you could tie it back to the post-Cold War era as the world has changed, some of you can tie it back to the evolution of China since the post-Nixon era and China's rise as an economic power, and now as a growing military power—that as we participated in those changes, we were promoting relations, we were promoting economic activity, we were promoting trade with a lot of these emerging economies, and we just kind of lost track of how we were doing. And as a result, things got a little bit out of balance.

And I think that's—as you hear the President talk about it, that's what he really speaks about, is: Look, things have gotten out of balance, and these are really important relationships to us and they're really important alliances, but we've got to bring them back into balance.

So it doesn't have to come at the expense of others, but it does have to come at an engagement with others. And so as we're building our policies around those notions, that's what we want to support. But at the end of it, it is strengthening our national security and promoting economic prosperity for the American people, and we do that, again, with a lot of partners.

Now, I think it's important to also remember that guiding all of our foreign policy actions are our fundamental values: our values around freedom, human dignity, the way people are treated. Those are our values. Those are not our policies; they're values. And the reason it's important, I think, to keep that well understood is that policies can change. They do change. They should change. Policies change to adapt to the—our values never change. They're constant throughout all of this.

And so I think the real challenge many of us have as we think about constructing our policies and carrying out our policies is: How do we represent our values? And in some circumstances, if you condition our national security efforts on someone adopting our values, we probably can't achieve our national security goals or our national security interests.

[On North Korea:] In evaluating that, what was important to us and to me to understand was, first, where are our allies? And so, engaging with our allies and ensuring that our allies and we see the situation the same—our allies in South Korea, our allies in Japan.

And then, secondly, it was to engage with the other regional powers as to how do they see it. And so it was useful and helpful to have the Chinese and now the Russians articulate clearly that their policy is unchanged. They—their policy is a denuclearized Korean Peninsula. And of course we did our part many years ago. We took all the nuclear weapons out of South Korea. So now we have a shared objective, and that's very useful, from which you then build out your policy approaches and your strategies .

So we are being very open and transparent about our intentions, and we're asking our partners around the world to please take actions on your own. We want you to control how that happens. We're not trying to control it for you, but we have an expectation of what you will do. So we're putting that pressure on. We are preparing additional sanctions, if it turns out North Korea's actions warrant additional sanctions. We're hopeful that the regime in North Korea will think about this and come to a conclusion that there's another way to the future. We know they have—they're—they aspire to nuclear weapons because it's the regime's belief it's the only way they can secure their future.

We are clear—we've been clear to them this is not about regime change, this is not about regime collapse, this is not about an accelerated reunification of the peninsula, this is not about us looking for an excuse to come north of the 38th Parallel. So we're trying to be very, very clear and resolute in our message to them that your future security and economic prosperity can only be achieved through your following your commitments to denuclearize.

And then if I pivoted over to China, because it really took us directly to our China foreign policy, we really had to assess China's situation, as I said, from the Nixon era up to where we find things today, and we saw a bit of an inflection point with the Beijing Olympics. Those were enormously successful for China. They kind of put China on the map, and China really began to feel its oats about that time, and rightfully.

They have achieved a lot. They moved 500 million Chinese people out of poverty into middle class status. They've still got a billion more they need to move.

So China has its own challenges, and we want to work with them and be mindful of what they're dealing with in the context of our relationship.

So we are using the entree of the visit in Mar-a-Lago, which was heavy on some issues with North Korea but also heavy on a broader range of issues. And what we've asked the Chinese to do is … to take a fresh look at where is this relationship going to be 50 years from now, because I think we have an opportunity to define that.

This speech by the American Secretary of State indicates that there is a potential to forge the kind of partnership that Lyndon and Helga LaRouche have long advocated between the United States, Russia, and China which will make it possible to address most of the world's conflicts from a higher standpoint. The fact that none of the major news media in the United States have bothered to inform the American people of their government's expressed intent reveals that the British—Liberal-Imperialist owners of the press and "public opinion" consider this potential a grave threat to their terminally bankrupt system. They would much prefer global war.

As Schiller recognized and expressed in his remarkable short poem "Columbus," translated above, it is a quality of genius to be able to see the future, and to know and understand the laws of nature well enough to know that this potential "dream" will exist in reality. In *The Earth's Next Fifty Years*, in the section entitled "Toward a Second Treaty of Westphalia: The Coming Eurasian World," LaRouche writes the following, which if taken seriously, will allow us to realize the potential now before us.

In statecraft, as in physical science, the primary challenge and responsibility, is the thinker's ability, and willingness, to adopt an emotionally driven sense of moral responsibility for the long-term effects on future society, of the choices we make in the short term of the here and now. Competent statecraft requires that we not make the potentially fatal mistake of even many figures who are otherwise gifted and well-meaning; we must not permit strategy (i.e., policy) to be driven by tactics, as does an otherwise able commander in battles who wins the day, but loses the war.[1]

Then, once we have accepted that requirement, we must, as I shall also show here, now match that view of an integrated, millennial process of European civilization against the challenge of building a secure future for our planet, through new forms of relationship with what are broadly classed as Asian culture. Now, after thousands of years, precisely that challenge now faces us all, as never, in comparable degree, in history before this time.

---

1. An example is the case of the qualified professional U.S. military commanders sent to fight an anti-Constitutional, unjustified war in Iraq, a so-called "war without an exit strategy," which the U.S. forces are dying now, ultimately to lose. So, in Indo-China, U.S. forces won the battles, but ultimately, inevitably, lost the war. The highest expression of strategy in military affairs, is, as General Douglas MacArthur did often in the Pacific, to win the war without fighting unnecessary battles, thus even causing the potential adversary to praise the ultimate outcome.

On the Occasion of The 50th Anniversary of the Belt and Road Summit—2067

Journal Entry from a Scientist Working in the Moon's Permanent Research City

by Kesha Rogers

May 14, 2067

Today is the 50-year anniversary of the day when President Trump surprised the world and attended the Silk Road Forum in Beijing, China—thus changing the entire course of history. Looking back from my vantage point, living and working in Selenopolis, to where we have come since this pivotal shift, our progress is so remarkable that it seems important to write it down so that others can remember it, and relive the path by which such a beautiful world as I now live in, came into existence.

It has been five years since mankind successfully diverted a large comet from impacting planet Earth. By uniting the space programs of the world into a global mission to use a thermonuclear-powered rocket to launch a fleet of satellites quickly out to the comet, and deploy an array of lasers and explosives to slow down its trajectory, the possible extinction of civilization was averted through the collaborative scientific and engineering prowess of the entire world.

Seven years ago, the Democratic Republic of the Congo became the last nation on Earth to enter the Space Age, graduating its first class of astronauts. We have now brought the entire human species into a new era. What was once one of the most desolate and war-ravaged places on the planet, has now become a hub of scientific and artistic genius. I am pleased to share my workstation with one of these men, an atomic physicist from that same Democratic Republic of the Congo.

It has been eleven years since the last human family rose above the poverty line. Global life expectancy is now over eighty-nine years. Previously "incurable" diseases like cancer, AIDS, and many more, have been basically eradicated because of the tremendous number of new scientists who are graduating from countries that, only two or three generations ago, had the highest rates of infant mortality, drug abuse, ethnic violence, and terrorism.

It has been twenty-five years since the completion of NAWAPA XXI (an upgraded 21st Century version of the original North American Water and Power Alliance, originally proposed over one hundred years ago, in 1964). As a result, the arable land in the United States has quadrupled, and farmers from California's Imperial Valley to the corn belt of the Midwest have been able to feed the entire country, with surpluses that have mitigated famines all over the world. Since that time, as a result of our sophistication in weather forecasting by our grasp of solar, geological, biospheric, and cosmic interactions, we have been able to prevent dozens of hurricanes from making landfall, and hundreds of earthquakes from destroying cities. Drought is now a thing of the past.

It has been thirty-nine years since the completion of the World Land Bridge, a global network of magnetically levitated, high-speed rail systems. I remember, when I was a little girl, my parents taking our family on this train, from our home in Houston, all the way around the world and back again for our Summer vacation. We traveled from Texas to Alaska and then across the Bering Strait down to China, to India, across to Egypt, down the African coast to South Africa, then up the opposite coast into Europe, then back across Russia, and after re-crossing the Bering Strait, continued down into central and South America, all the way to the Strait of Magellan. It was this trip that first inspired in me Schiller's idea of being a citizen of the world, even as I am a citizen of my own country. It had a permanent effect on my desire to explore, and is a big part of why I became a space scientist.

Forty-four years ago, scientists working around the planet finally discovered the secrets of thermonuclear fusion technology. This breakthrough is still celebrated as a global holiday, and I am proud to be part of the Helium-3 excavation team on Selenopolis, working to separate the He-3 from the lunar soil, as we prepare it for packaging in the regular cargo shipments to Earth.

It has been forty-eight years since the official dissolution of the British Empire, following the series of highly public, intergovernmental tribunals by the UN Security Council, and numerous independent state investigative hearings. The world was amazed, but not necessarily shocked, at the depth of penetration by what was then inadequately described as the "deep state" into every facet of life, in order to prop up the bankrupt financial predators who were intent on keeping the world in a state of permanent war, poverty, and backwardness. It had started two years earlier, after Congress had passed the aptly named "LaRouche Recovery Program of 2017," following the final bursting of the derivatives bubble, with the reinstatement of the Glass-Steagall Act.

All of this leads us to our anniversary of today. Fifty years ago, over one-hundred ten nations held a summit in Beijing, China, in the spirit of "win-win cooperation" that Chinese President Xi Jinping had defined as the basis for the New Silk Road. All the leading nations of the world participated, including then President Donald Trump—after a long battle by treasonous agents in the United States and British Empire, to keep the U.S.A. from joining in this pivotal event that changed the direction of humanity. All the progress we have seen since then, was basically unimaginable to most people alive at that time, because so much of the visionary leadership and growth our country experienced over one hundred years ago under President Kennedy, had been lost.

Before President Trump made the remarkable decision to attend the summit in Beijing—which is largely why I am here today at my beautiful workstation on the Moon—there was no guarantee that our country would even still exist today. The passage and implementation following that summit, of the recovery program of the United States, was key to taking power away from Wall Street and the free market criminals who insisted on a system of economy based on monetary speculation.

They were trying to warp our space program into a tourism scam, instead of the scientific powerhouse it has become today. Thank God that Glass-Steagall was reinstated, and that the evil Wall-Street money system was replaced with a real economy, in which the priority for credit is for it to be used to develop the physical economy with a mission for mankind in space. Everything that started at the New Silk Road Forum set into motion the new era of optimism and discovery that allowed me to be here today.

I must hurry and complete this entry, because I have to catch the nuclear space elevator to Mars. I have an interplanetary Chorus Practice to attend very soon. So I will finish, having described that historic month of May, fifty years ago.

www.ingramcontent.com/pod-product-compliance
Lightning Source LLC
Chambersburg PA
CBHW080833310526
45788CB00020B/3522